IMMERSION
Bible Studies:

HOSEA
JOEL
AMOS
OBADIAH
JONAH

Acknowledgments

Prophetic ministry is grounded in a gratitude for God's graceful presence in our lives and the world. In that spirit, I want to say thank you to several people. I am grateful to my father and mother, Everett and Loretta Epperly, for teaching me about the importance of the Bible and for raising me in a home where care for the marginalized was a way of life. I am grateful to John Akers and George "Shorty" Collins, who taught me the social dimensions of the gospel. I give thanks for Professor John Cobb, who showed me the relationship between theology, justice, and ecology.

I am ever grateful to my life partner, Kate Epperly, whose loving support has enabled me to live my theology on a daily basis. Finally, I dedicate this book to my two grandsons, Jack and James, who inspire me to work for a world in which every child has a healthy diet, adequate housing, education, healthcare, the ability to create new things and contribute to the beauty of the earth.

Praise for IMMERSION

"IMMERSION BIBLE STUDIES is a powerful tool in helping readers to hear God speak through Scripture and to experience a deeper faith as a result."
Adam Hamilton, author of *24 Hours That Changed the World*

"IMMERSION BIBLE STUDIES is a godsend for participants who desire sound Bible study yet feel they do not have large amounts of time for study and preparation. IMMERSION is concise. It is brief but covers the material well and leads participants to apply the Bible to life. IMMERSION is a wonderful resource for today's church."
Larry R. Baird, senior pastor of Trinity Grand Island United Methodist Church

"If you're looking for a deeper knowledge and understanding of God's Word, you must dive into IMMERSION BIBLE STUDIES. Whether in a group setting or as an individual, you will experience God and his unconditional love for each of us in a whole new way."
Pete Wilson, founding and senior pastor of Cross Point Church

"This beautiful series helps readers become fluent in the words and thoughts of God, for purposes of illumination, strength building, and developing a closer walk with the One who loves us so."
Laurie Beth Jones, author of *Jesus, CEO* and *The Path*

"I highly commend to you IMMERSION BIBLE STUDIES, which tells us what the Bible teaches and how to apply it personally."
John Ed Mathison, author of *Treasures of the Transformed Life*

IMMERSION
Bible Studies

HOSEA, JOEL, AMOS, OBADIAH, JONAH

Bruce Epperly

Abingdon Press

Nashville

HOSEA, JOEL, AMOS, OBADIAH, JONAH
IMMERSION BIBLE STUDIES
by Bruce Epperly

Copyright © 2013 by Abingdon Press

Library of Congress Cataloging-in-Publication Data

Epperly, Bruce Gordon.
  Hosea, Joel, Amos, Obadiah, Jonah / Bruce Epperly.
    pages cm. — (Immersion Bible studies)
  Includes bibliographical references and index.
  ISBN 978-1-4267-1639-3 (book - pbk. unsewn/adhesive casebound : alk.paper)
  1. Bible. Minor Prophets — Textbooks. I. Title.
  BS1560.E67 2013
  224'.906—dc23

                          2013010078

Editor: Josh Tinley
Leader Guide Writer: Josh Tinley

13 14 15 16 17 18 19 20 21 22—10 9 8 7 6 5 4 3 2 1

Manufactured in the United States of America

Contents

Review Team

Diane Blum
Pastor and Spiritual Director
Nashville, Tennessee

Susan Cox
Pastor
McMurry United Methodist Church
Claycomo, Missouri

Margaret Ann Crain
Professor of Christian Education
Garrett-Evangelical Theological Seminary
Evanston, Illinois

Nan Duerling
Curriculum Writer and Editor
Cambridge, Maryland

Paul Escamilla
Pastor and Writer
St. John's United Methodist Church
Austin, Texas

James Hawkins
Pastor and Writer
Smyrna, Delaware

Andrew Johnson
Professor of New Testament
Nazarene Theological Seminary
Kansas City, Missouri

Snehlata Patel
Pastor
Woodrow United Methodist Church
Staten Island, New York

Emerson B. Powery
Professor of New Testament
Messiah College
Grantham, Pennsylvania

Clayton Smith
Pastoral Staff
Church of the Resurrection
Leawood, Kansas

Harold Washington
Professor of Hebrew Bible
Saint Paul School of Theology
Kansas City, Missouri

Carol Wehrheim
Curriculum Writer and Editor
Princeton, New Jersey

IMMERSION BIBLE STUDIES

A fresh new look at the Bible, from beginning to end,
and what it means in your life.

Welcome to IMMERSION!

We've asked some of the leading Bible scholars, teachers, and pastors to help us with a new kind of Bible study. IMMERSION remains true to Scripture but always asks, "Where are you in your life? What do you struggle with? What makes you rejoice?" Then it helps you read the Scriptures to discover their deep, abiding truths. IMMERSION is about God and God's Word, and it is also about you—not just your thoughts, but your feelings and your faith.

In each study you will prayerfully read the Scripture and reflect on it. Then you will engage it in three ways:

Claim Your Story
Through stories and questions, think about your life, with its struggles and joys.

Enter the Bible Story
Explore Scripture and consider what God is saying to you.

Live the Story
Reflect on what you have discovered, and put it into practice in your life.

IMMERSION makes use of an exciting new translation of Scripture, the Common English Bible (CEB). The CEB and IMMERSION BIBLE STUDIES will offer adults:
- the emotional expectation to find the love of God
- the rational expectation to find the knowledge of God
- reliable, genuine, and credible power to transform lives
- clarity of language

Whether you are using the Common English Bible or another translation, IMMERSION BIBLE STUDIES will offer a refreshing plunge into God's Word, your life, and your life with God.

INTRODUCTION

The prophets invite us to enter the hardscrabble world of power structures, political decision-making, and economic uncertainty. Hosea, Joel, Amos, Obadiah, and Jonah may upset us with their forceful language and judgment of the wealthy and powerful. These prophets demanded justice and let no one off the hook.

The prophets did much more than scold God's people. There is hope in their writings; but this hope can be realized only through changed hearts, a devotion to justice and righteousness, and the unexpected surprises of God's grace. Their prophetic words suggest that we must go through the "darkest valley" (Psalm 23:4) before we claim God's land of promise and fulfillment. But even when we fall short and suffer the consequences of our actions, God remains our companion and does everything possible to guide us toward paths of healing and righteousness.

Our culture has a tendency to conflate prophecy and fortune-telling. But the biblical prophets seldom foretold the future. Rather, they have a keen sense of cause and effect when it comes to the affairs of people and nations. Their visions of the future come with an awareness of the freedom God gives us to change course in response to God's call and echo Deuteronomy 30:19: "I have set life and death, blessing and curse before you. Now choose life—so that you and your descendents will live—by loving the LORD your God, by obeying his voice, and clinging to him."

The prophets voice a concern for the poor and vulnerable that reflects God's own concern for people on the margins of society. They cry out against injustice because God hears the cry of the needy. The prophets' pain and anger toward injustice mirrors God's pain and, dare we say, anger whenever one individual is lost due to human neglect, abuse, or oppression. They hope for a new tomorrow because God is alive and moving in the world, wholeness for God's people in Israel and Judah and for all of the nations of the world.

A journey through the prophetic writings isn't always comfortable. It holds our values and priorities up to the mirror of divine justice and calls us to repentance. Despite its challenge to our way of life, reading the prophets is rewarding because it invites us to spiritual transformation and companionship with God in the quest to heal all of God's creation. The prophets' challenging words reflect their love for humankind and for God's will.

1.

The Prophet as Mystic and Voice for God

Hosea—Jonah

Claim Your Story

The Pew Forum on Religion and Public Life reports that nearly half of North Americans claim to have had mystical experiences. This represents a sharp increase from 1962, when only 22 percent of the population reported having spiritually transforming experiences. According to the current study, 40 percent of mainline Christians report spiritual awakenings compared with 37 percent of non-Hispanic Roman Catholics, 71 percent of white evangelicals, and 71 percent of African-American Protestants. While the study does not specify the exact nature of such experiences, perhaps these spiritual awakenings include near death experiences, hearing whispers from God, speaking in tongues, having a sense of oneness with God, and experiencing feelings of amazement and wonder in the presence of nature. If you are attending church this Sunday, the person sitting next to you may be a mystic. And you may even be a mystic yourself.

Each of the five books that you will be studying describes encounters in which God directly addresses the prophet. Whether it is the fleeing Jonah, vindictive Obadiah, jealous Hosea, confrontational Amos, or hopeful Joel, each has a life-changing encounter in which God calls him to speak words of judgment and hope to Israel's Northern or Southern Kingdoms and, by extension, to us today. Their authority comes from the One who called them and whose message they convey to a wayward nation.

We live in a time and place where people make all sorts of spiritual claims, from faith healings to near-death experiences to messages from deceased persons to encounters with spiritual beings. What are we to make of such mystical experiences? Is there any way that we can evaluate claims to come from a divine or spiritual encounters? Regardless, the prevalence of mystical experiences forces us to consider that human experience is not limited to the five senses.

Often when we hear the word *prophecy* or *prophet*, we think of these mystical experiences and spiritual encounters. And many biblical prophets sometimes reported other-worldly experiences; they spoke very concrete messages directed to concrete people in concrete situations. These messages related to business practices, foreign policy, and authentic worship, among other topics.

Enter the Bible Story

I must confess that I become a little nervous whenever I hear someone say, "God told me," or "I heard God saying to me." While I believe that God communicates with humankind, I am dubious about our ability to determine the exact nature of God's messages to us. As many theologians have noted, revelation always requires a receiver. There is no revelation in general given to all human beings. Rather, inspiration comes to specific human beings in specific historical and cultural settings.

Too often, declarations such as "God spoke to me" or "I am doing God's will" have been invoked by authoritarian leaders or others who want to justify acts of violence or oppression. Regardless of the recipient, God's revelation is always conditioned by human limitations, such as sin and self-interest.

The prophets of Israel would have recognized the historical and cultural nature of their revelatory experiences, but they also spoke with a passion grounded in their belief that they had truly encountered the Living God, who had appointed them messengers to the nation's political, religious, and economic leaders. Listen to these words invoked in the five biblical texts that you are about to study. They are grounded in the prophet's confidence in that God speaks to human beings:

The LORD's word came to Hosea, Beeri's
son, in the days of Judah's Kings Uzziah,
Jotham, Ahaz, and Hezekiah, and in
the days of Israel's King Jeroboam,
Joash's son. (Hosea 1:1)

When the LORD first spoke through
Hosea. ... (Hosea 1:2)

The LORD's word that came to Joel,
Pethuel's son. ... (Joel 1:1)

Yet even now, says the LORD,
    return to me with all your hearts. ...
(Joel 2:12)

The LORD proclaims. ... (Amos 1:3)

Hear this word that the LORD has spoken
against you, people of Israel. ... (Amos 3:1)

The vision of Obadiah,
    the LORD God proclaims
        concerning Edom:
We have heard a message
    from the LORD—
a messenger has been sent
    among the nations. ... (Obadiah 1)

The LORD's word came to Jonah,
Amittai's son. ... (Jonah 1:1)

The LORD's word came to Jonah a second
time. ... (Jonah 3:1)

Across the Testaments

Revelation and Mysticism in the New Testament

The New Testament is a library of mystical and revelatory experiences. Voices and visions emerging from the human encounter with God abound. On Pentecost, Jesus' first followers experience a mighty wind and tongues of flame. Filled with the Holy Spirit, they testify to God's revelation in Jesus of Nazareth, breaking down barriers of ethnicity, nationality, age, gender, and status (Acts 2:1-21). Saul, who was busy rounding up and arresting Christians, receives a vision of the Risen Christ on the road to Damascus. Ananias receives a corresponding vision instructing him to welcome and mentor the former persecutor (Acts 9:1-16). Peter and Cornelius have visions that bring them together to expand the Gospel message to the Gentile world (Acts 10:1-48). Paul receives a vision that sends him to Philippi where he establishes a congregation (Acts 16:6-10).

The early church believed that God sends messages to human beings. These messages are not meant for individual ecstasy but to expand God's influence in history and to invite people to personal and corporate transformation.

As we begin this study, we first need to explore the nature and source of the prophet's authority. We will consider the following issues: 1) the source of prophetic authority, 2) the identity and character of the One for whom the prophet speaks, 3) the nature of the prophet's experience of God's call, and 4) the meaning of prophetic inspiration, for people today.[1]

The Source of Prophetic Authority

The biblical tradition affirms that all creatures reveal divine wisdom and intentionality. God's presence throughout the world inspires the psalmist to write: "Shout triumphantly to the LORD, all the earth!" (Psalm 100:1); "Let every living thing praise the LORD" (Psalm 150:6); "Heaven is declaring God's glory; the sky is proclaiming his handiwork" (Psalm 19:1); and "From the rising of the sun to where it sets, God, the LORD God, speaks, calling out to the earth" (Psalm 50:1). Scripture also asserts that God shapes our lives, institutions, and the broad arc of history.

According to the prophets, God takes the initiative to reach out to humanity. God is concerned about our joys and sorrows, rejoices in our triumphs, and mourns our grief. God calls Abraham and Sarah to leave the familiarity of Haran to sojourn to a promised land. Despite the couple's infertility, God promises them a child whose descendants will form a great nation. Through a dream, God presents Jacob with his vocation. Through a voice speaking through a burning bush, God awakens Moses to his vocation as the liberator and leader of his people. Later, God reveals the Law to Moses on Mt. Sinai. God continues to speak to humankind through persons set apart by their experience of God's call—persons such as Amos, Hosea, Obadiah, Joel, Jonah, Isaiah, Ezekiel, Micah, and Jeremiah.

The New Testament writers describe this same God taking the initiative in encounters with Mary, Joseph, Paul, and Peter (among others). Those of us who call ourselves Christians believe that God's ultimate and most intimate revelation occurred in the life, teaching, ministry, death, and resurrection of Jesus of Nazareth.

Although Scripture recognizes that God is present everywhere and can communicate with anyone at any time, it also affirms that God's presence is not a homogenous, neutral energy distributed evenly throughout creation. The profoundly personal God speaks intimately and personally to individuals and communities. God can act and speak in ways that reveal God's vision for particular historical situations, using the gifts of particular historical persons. The Hebraic prophets and their followers believed that God called them to speak words of warning and hope to the people. Their authority came from their affirmation that God communicated God's intentions to them.

Historically, the word *prophet* is a Greek translation of the Hebraic *nabi*, which can be defined as "one who is called by God or one who delivers a message from another." The authority of the prophet came from the One who spoke to him or her. The prophet's message, embedded in a particular historical situation for the purpose of calling the nation to a new self-understanding, is not just his own, but a revelation of God's desire for humankind and the world. When the prophetic texts say, "The LORD said to [Hosea]" (Hosea 1:4), they really mean it; and the nation had better listen!

The prophetic books do not get into theological explanations of how God communicated to God's messengers. They simply say that God called Amos or Hosea, or—if we are to let the prophets speak for themselves—"God called me." This sense of prophetic authority is best seen in the unexpected calls of Isaiah and Jeremiah. Isaiah proclaims: "In the year of King Uzziah's death, I saw the Lord sitting on a high and exalted throne" (Isaiah 6:1). Although "all the earth is filled with God's glory" (Isaiah 6:3), God has a specific word for the awe-filled prophet-to-be: "Whom should I send, and who will go for us?" Although he is free to say no, Isaiah stammers, "I am here; send me" (Isaiah 6:8).

Concerned that he is too inexperienced to share God's message, Jeremiah receives God's assurance: " 'Don't be afraid of them, because I am with you to rescue you.... I'm putting my words in your mouth' " (Jeremiah 1:8, 9). When the religious establishment questions Amos's credentials, he recalls God's intimate movements in his own life, calling him from anonymity to prophesy to the centers of political and religious power:

> I am not a prophet, nor am I a prophet's
> son; but I am a shepherd, and a trimmer
> of sycamore trees. But the LORD took
> me from shepherding the flock, and the
> LORD said to me, "Go, prophesy to my
> people Israel." (Amos 7:14-15)

His encounter with God gives Amos the courage to say to Amaziah, the priest of Bethel, whose education and credentials dwarfed the prophet's, "Now then hear the LORD's word." The prophet makes no claims to be the source of revelation; rather, he is God's spokesperson, compelled by the profundity of his encounter to share God's vision in this time and place.

The One for Whom the Prophet Speaks

At the heart of the prophet's experience is a life-changing confrontation with the living, historical, and relational God. God—Creator of heaven and earth, who spoke to the patriarchs Abraham, Isaac, and Jacob; surprised Sarah with a child; brought the captives out of Israel; and established their identity as a nation with the commandments of Sinai— is the focal point of everything the prophet says.

Highly personal in nature, prophetic spirituality avoids two extremes: pantheism and deism. Pantheism identifies God with the totality of experience; it affirms that God and the world are one reality, without distinction. God is the whole of which we are parts. Pantheism has inspired certain mystics to proclaim, "I am God," as a result of their belief that the divine and human are one reality. Although pantheists celebrate our connection with all things, there is little moral edge in pantheism. There is little confrontation between the "is" and the "ought." Life in its totality, good and evil, reflects the wisdom of the Whole.

In contrast to the homogeneity characteristic of pantheism, deism holds that God is completely separated from the ongoing processes of human and cosmic history. Like a clockmaker, God sets the universe in motion, establishing its fundamental laws, and then lets it run according to its own machinations. Deism leaves the world entirely in the hands of human actors: We have come of age and have the whole world in our hands.

In an attempt to join deism with the biblical vision of God's action in history, some Christians describe God's presence as occasional and supernatural. Most of the time, they believe, God remains at the sidelines of history and nature, except when God intervenes in response to a human crisis, punishing human immorality or performing a miracle of deliverance. These "acts of God" are interventions from the outside to change the course of history, which, otherwise, is only indirectly influenced by God. While the prophets have a strong sense of God's activity in history and nature, this activity is seen as constant rather than arbitrary in nature.

The prophetic tradition also challenges Aristotle's vision of God as "the unmoved mover," completely unaffected by the world of change. Perfection, according to Aristotle and his non-Christian and Christian disciples, is best understood in terms of God's changeless eternity. God's relationship to the world is reflected in God's eternal vision of all that will occur and God's determination of every event in advance. Nothing new happens to the God of changeless perfection; any change in God would be from perfection to imperfection. From this perspective, the God-world relationship is one-sided, unilateral; God shapes but is not influenced by our transitory and imperfect lives.

In contrast to all three viewpoints, the prophetic tradition asserts that God is historical, relational, and intimate. God has a stake in history as it unfolds. God's vision is reflected in the affairs of persons and nations. God liberates the children of Israel from Egyptian captivity, guides them through the wilderness, and provides a homeland for them. God judges the rulers of the earth according to their concern for justice. God is passionate and creative. God hears our prayers and responds to our repentance.

Rabbi Abraham Joshua Heschel describes the relationship of God, the world, and humankind in terms of the "divine pathos." Although God exerts tremendous power in world events as the force behind drought, plague, and invasion, God is also affected by what goes on in the world. God feels the pain of the vulnerable and experiences anguish in response to Israel's infidelity. God's sovereignty is balanced by God's intimate care for God's people.

Life's Details Matter to God

What happens in the seats of power is important because political and economic decisions can be matters of life and death to thousands, if not millions, of people. Turning away from God not only undermines temple worship, it also leads to injustice in human affairs. Every human being created in God's image is of significant value. The God of the prophets, like Jesus of Nazareth, weeps over Jerusalem and pities the lost souls of Nineveh. The depth God's sorrow for human waywardness is expressed in the words of Hosea:

> When Israel was a child, I loved him,
> and out of Egypt I called my son.
> The more I called them,
> the further they went from me;
> they kept sacrificing to the Baals,
> and they burned incense to idols.
> Yet it was I who taught Ephraim to walk;
> I took them up in my arms,
> but they did not know that
> I healed them.

> I led them
> > with bands of human kindness,
> > with cords of love.
> I treated them like those
> > who lift infants to their cheeks;
> > I bent down to them and fed them....
> How can I give up on you, Ephraim?...
> My hearts winces within me;
> > my compassion
> > grows warm and tender.
> (Hosea 11:1-4, 8)

Hosea, who vacillates between love and anger in relationship to his unfaithful wife Gomer, comes to view his life as part of a greater drama: the drama of God's passionate love, frustration, and eventual redemption of God's people.

The prophetic vision of God is grounded in relationship to One who communicates with human beings. When the prophet shouts words of condemnation, his judgment is conditioned by an equally profound experience of the passionate heart of a God who yearns for communion with Israel.

The Prophet's Experience of God's Call

The prophets were spiritual leaders and mystics whose encounters with God gave them a mission to call the nation to God's ways. God spoke to them and through them about issues of economics, political decision-making, foreign policy, and care for the most vulnerable members of society. In the words of Rabbi Heschel, the prophet's mind is preoccupied with "the concrete activities of history rather than the timeless issues of thought."[2]

The nature of the mystic's quest depends on the object of her or his search. Those who see the ultimate reality as timeless and impersonal, as did the philosopher and Christian mystic Plotinus, seek to journey from the "alone to the Alone." The goal of spiritual practices is to go beyond the transitory world of diversity and conflict to experience the ultimate calm of dissolving, like a drop of water, into the great ocean of Being.

Other Christians, not necessarily of a mystical variety, see the point of earthly existence as escaping this earthly veil of tears to experience eternal rest in God's heavenly abode.

The Hebraic prophets seem far too concerned with this world to please those whose primary goal is unity with the Ultimate or a heavenly reward. The prophets are embedded in this world; they have some "skin in the game," because their future well-being depends on the nation's turning back to God. Their justice-oriented, this-worldly spirituality finds its inspiration in a justice-oriented, this-worldly God, who is beyond yet always involved in the hardscrabble world of politics and economics.

The prophet's experience of God is ethical and relational in nature. The prophet may even challenge God's decisions when he or she petitions God to change God's mind, pleading for mercy for the nation and deliverance from divine wrath in the form of avenging foes (Amos 7:1-6). In the person-to-Person relationship of the prophet and God, the prophet actively seeks the nation's well-being by speaking for God in public and, at times, arguing with God in private. The prophet is not a mere instrument of revelation but an active partner in God's quest to heal the world.

The Relevance of the Prophetic Experience for Us

Spirituality is not an escape from the world. Our encounters with God draw us into the complexities of politics and economics. In contrast to the individualism of much contemporary religion and spiritual practice, prophetic spirituality always aims at the well-being of the community. While he or she trusts in God's ultimate transformation of history, the prophet lives and works in the present. Justice in God's world, right now, is our calling, because it matters to God.

Prophets never pretend to know the future in its entirety. They can foresee the impact that economic, political, and religious decisions will have on the future; and they know whether a nation or people is heading in the direction God intends. But prophets are clear that the future hasn't been determined yet and that God will have the final word.

Live the Story

Recent years have seen a rise in the number of people who describe themselves as "spiritual but not religious." In a 2010 survey conducted by LifeWay Christian Resources, 72 percent of young adults between the ages of 18 and 29 identify themselves as such.[3] People in this group tend to associate *spirituality* with freedom, creativity, tolerance, and *vitality* and *religion* with legalism, intolerance, dogmatism, and disdain for science. Those who identify as spiritual but not religious often see religious institutions as lifeless, inflexible vestiges of a bygone era. In contrast, they understand spirituality as encouraging freedom, creativity, variety, and novelty.

Not everyone feels that religion and spirituality are mutually exclusive. Some Christians have begun to describe themselves as "spiritual and religious." Many of these Christians find their inspiration in the Hebraic prophets; Jesus' ministry of healing and hospitality; the lively unhindered faith described in Acts of the Apostles; and modern spiritual leaders such as Dorothy Day, Mother Teresa, Martin Luther King, Howard Thurman, Dietrich Bonhoeffer, and Desmond Tutu, whose encounters with God inspired them to become agents in social transformation.

As you look at your congregation, where does it stand on the continuum of spirituality? Do people take spiritual practices such as prayer and meditation seriously? Are people comfortable with the possibility that God might speak to them or that our prayers can be effective, healing body, mind, and spirit? Would you describe your church and its members as "religious but not spiritual" (rule and ritual oriented, concerned with externals and propriety in worship, doctrine, and administration); "spiritual but not religious" (experience-oriented and suspicious of institutional frameworks); or "spiritual and religious" (committed to a flexible, innovative, experiential faith that joins contemplation and social action)? What spiritual practices might you adopt to become more attentive to God's call in your life?

1. My interpretation of the prophet's encounter with God is influenced by Abraham Joshua Heschel's magisterial text *The Prophets* (New York: Harper and Row, 1962).

2. From *The Prophets*, by Abraham Joshua Heschel (New York: Harper and Row, 1962), page 5.

3. From *http://www.usatoday.com/news/religion/2010-04-27-1Amillfaith27_ST_N.htm* (3-18-13).

2.

Theology, Ethics, and Politics in the Prophetic Writings

Hosea—Jonah

Claim Your Story

On August 28, 1963, Martin Luther King, Jr., delivered his landmark "I Have a Dream" speech at the Lincoln Memorial. King's speech was grounded in the social, political, and spiritual message of the Hebrew prophets. King cited Amos 5:24 when he proclaimed, "No, no, we are not satisfied, and we will not be satisfied until 'justice rolls down like waters, and righteousness like a mighty stream'" (Amos 5:24).

Like the prophets of Israel and Judah, King shared his dream of "the beloved community," based on his understanding of God's Shalom, or wholeness for all creation. He told the crowd gathered in front of the Lincoln Memorial, in Washington, D.C., on August 28, 1963, that he had "a dream." His dream was of a racially unified nation in which black children and white children could join hands as "sisters and brothers" and where people would be judged and treated according to their character, not their skin color. In describing his dream, King drew from the prophet Isaiah, who offered this vision: "Every valley will be raised up, and every mountain and hill will be flattened.... The LORD's glory will appear, and all humanity will see it together" (Isaiah 40:4-5). In King's dream, as in Isaiah's vision, justice prevails over discrimination and inequality.[1]

A few months earlier, King responded to a group of clergy who challenged his integration of religion and social change. In the midst of a mighty struggle to rid our nation of racial and economic injustice, I have heard many pastors say: "Those are social issues, with which the gospel has no real concern." And I have watched many churches commit themselves to a completely otherworldly religion which makes a strange, un-biblical distinction between body and soul, between the sacred and secular.[2]

The Hebrew prophets saw the nation's religious life as intimately related to issues of economics, justice, and care for the vulnerable. The prophetic writings challenge us to consider the following questions: Is it appropriate for God's people to take sides on political and social issues? How should Christians respond to political and social differences within the church (for example, differing opinions on abortion and contraception, economic policy, care for the environment, healthcare accessibility, and marriage)? Is there more than one Christian position on the major ethical issues of our time? Is our primary responsibility to care for persons in this lifetime or prepare them for eternal life?

Enter the Bible Story

When we enter the world of the prophets, we have to be prepared to be uncomfortable. No nation has ever fully lived up to the prophetic dream of justice rolling down like waters. All nations live under God's judgment for their treatment of the poor and vulnerable. To the prophets, our sacred principles of private property and profit-making are subservient to the needs of our less fortunate brothers and sisters. In the rhetoric of the prophetic religion, there is no separation of religion, politics, and economics.

We will explore the relationship of ethics and economics in the prophets by considering the themes of: 1) creation and ethics, 2) covenant and ethics, 3) the ethics of blessing, 4) the prophetic challenge to the rich and powerful, and 5) the call to turn to God.

Creation and Ethics

God brought order and beauty out of chaos and created a universe that is blessed and good. Human and non-human life is valuable and good; all creatures are able to praise God (Genesis 1:1–2:4; Psalm 148–150). Marriage, sexuality, and childbirth are holy (Genesis 1:28). Human beings—male and female—are created in God's image (Genesis 1:26-28). Although humans have a unique place in creation, Scripture constantly reminds us, "The earth is the LORD's and everything in it" (Psalm 24:1). We are created co-creators.

Prophetic ethics takes seriously "the image of God" as a defining characteristic of every human life. Anything that violates another human being is a sin against God. In describing God's concern for justice, Rabbi Abraham Joshua Heschel asserts, "Israel's distress was more than a human tragedy. With Israel's distress came the affliction of God, His displacement, His homelessness in the land, in the world."[3] Amos' denunciation of dishonest business practices is based on belief that the poor are created in God's image (Amos 2:6-7).

What we do today in our care of our human and non-human companions is the heart of worship, spirituality, and ethics. Rabbi Heschel says, "Instead of dealing with timeless issues of being and becoming, of matter and form, of definitions and demonstrations, [the prophet] is thrown into orations about widows and orphans, about the corruption of judges, and affairs of the marketplace. . . . The prophets take us into the streets."[4]

The minute details of business practices and political decisions matter to the prophets because they matter to God. Every decision involves choosing life or death, physically or spiritually, for ourselves and for others.

Covenant and Ethics

Every nation has a story. In his "I Have a Dream" speech, King invokes the ideals of life, liberty, and the pursuit of happiness, which are celebrated in the story of the United States of America. On national holidays, citizens of the United States recall pilgrim journeys, the fight for freedom, the bounty of our land, and its special place as a "city on a hill" inspiring other lands to dream of freedom and democracy. But the American story also inspires critique, when the nation fails to fulfill its vision of justice and equality for large segments of the population.

The Hebrews saw themselves as intimate participants in God's story of salvation. They traced their history back to the patriarchs (Abraham,

Isaac, and Jacob) and the Exodus from Egypt and saw themselves as chosen by God to be a holy people. They did not earn their status, nor could they take it for granted. In response to God's unmerited love, God's people must love and care for one another (Hosea 13:1-5).

God's covenant with the Hebrews, as recorded in Torah, or Law, was a way of life in which the people affirmed their relationship with God and one another. Abiding by God's covenant brought joy and prosperity, while turning away from God led to sorrow and destruction (Hosea 9:15-17; 13:1-9; 14:1-3). As God's beloved, the children of Israel were to be light unto the nations, living by a different set of values and ethical practices than their neighbors. Virtually every aspect of life, from diet to business practices and behavior toward strangers, pertains to our relationship with God and is grounded in God's commandment to the children of Israel:

"I am the LORD your God. You must keep yourselves holy and be holy, because I am holy" (Leviticus 11:44). Covenant is a gift; but it is also an invitation to a new way of life, characterized by justice, equality, and care for the least of these.

Blessing and Ethics

To be blessed is to receive God's favor, which is not merely the pronouncement of a word of affirmation but the infusion of divine power, energy, and care. God blesses creation, humankind, and the sabbath, making time and space holy and blessed.

Abraham and Sarah received God's blessing as they begin their adventure toward a new land. God proclaimed, "I will make of you a great nation and I will bless you. I will make your name respected, and you will be a blessing" (Genesis 12:2). Later, after dreaming of a ladder of angels, Abraham's grandson Jacob received a blessing from the God of his father and grandfather: "I will give you and your descendants the land upon which you are lying. . . . Every family of the earth will be blessed because of you and your descendants" (Genesis 28:13, 14). Many Christians know the blessing that God gives to Moses and Aaron to pronounce upon the children of Israel:

> The LORD bless you and keep you.
> The LORD make his face shine on you
> and be gracious to you.
> The LORD lift up his face to you
> and grant you peace.
> (Numbers 6:24-27)

We are blessed to be a blessing. Implicit in God's blessing of creation, humankind, and the children of Israel is an ethic of blessing where every encounter is an opportunity to bless another person. When we bless one another, placing God at the center of our blessing, we flourish in mind, body, and spirit. When we turn away from the Source of All Blessings, we wither and die as individuals and nations. The prophets challenged behaviors that curse other people by threatening the well-being of widows, orphans, small farmers, and artisans. The prophetic call is to return to God's way of blessing so that everyone may enjoy divine abundance.

Prophetic Challenge to the Rich and Powerful

Although the prophets were often perceived as spiritual killjoys, their message was grounded in a positive vision of personal and social ethics. The prophetic spirit resounds in the words of Micah 6:8:

> He has told you, human one,
> what is good and
> what the LORD requires from you:
> to do justice, embrace faithful love,
> and walk humbly with your God.

The prophets recognized that the wealthy and powerful have primary responsibility for ensuring the well-being of the nation. The prophets asserted that those who controlled access to power, money, work, and property had an inherent and non-negotiable responsibility to seek good and not evil in the conduct of business and government. Decisions that had a negative impact on the nation's most vulnerable people could not be dismissed as "just business."

About the Christian Faith

The Social Gospel Movement

With the rise of industrialism and the shift in population from farms to cities, many Christians became concerned about widespread poverty among urban dwellers. Moreover, they saw the working conditions in most factories as a threat to the dignity, health, and family life of laborers. Religious leaders such as George Washington Gladden and Walter Rauschenbusch challenged the profit motive of big business. If profit is the only criteria of success, then anything that gets in the way of profit is detrimental to industry, including safe working conditions, fair salaries, vacations, reasonable hours, compensation for injuries, and secure retirement plans. Following the prophets, Social Gospel leaders saw sin as corporate as well as individual. Corporations must be challenged to be ethical in their treatment of workers, product safety, and working conditions. According to the Social Gospel, profit-making must be balanced with ethical responsibility to create healthy communities and just economic structures. Many practices we currently take for granted—such as worker compensation, safe working conditions, health insurance, and social security—were at the heart of the Social Gospel movement.

For prophets, nothing is just business, everything is spiritual and personal. As Rabbi Heschel proclaims: "To us a simple act of injustice—cheating in business, exploitation of the poor—is slight; to the prophets, a disaster. . . . a threat to the world."[5] Old Testament scholar Bruce Birch concurs: "The biblical word is clear: We cannot seek our salvation without seeking that of our neighbor, and we can't minister to the anguish of our neighbor's soul without ministering to the suffering of our neighbor's body."[6] In an interdependent world, everything we do matters not only to our neighbor but also to God.

The prophetic word against the wealthy and powerful is not a condemnation of these people but a call to conversion so that they too may be restored to spiritual health. Those who profit from injustice or put reputation before love of neighbor will damage their own souls. While the prophets side with the vulnerable in economic and political matters, their message is also intended to restore the spiritual health and personal well-being of those in power. "Seek the LORD and live" is their cry to rich and poor alike (Amos 5:4-6).

From the prophetic point of view, seeking God means pursuing justice and fairness, speaking the truth in love, and insuring that the most vulnerable people in society can meet their basic needs. Amos challenges Amaziah, the priest of Bethel, to call the powerful to justice (Amos 7:10-17). The wealthy and powerful can experience authentic fellowship with God, but their renewed relationship with God requires repentance and a commitment to justice for all people. These are hard words for any generation to hear, but they are words of eternal life—echoing from Amos to Jesus and contemporaries such as Martin Luther King, Jr.; Dorothy Day; Oscar Romero; and Desmond Tutu.

The Call to Turn to God

The situation was grave for the Northern and Southern Kingdoms of Israel. They had turned away from God by worshiping wooden idols, cheating in business, and neglecting the poor. This rejection of God and God's people led to economic and political chaos. The survival of Israel was in jeopardy. Indeed, both kingdoms were eventually overrun by foreign powers. Still, the prophets presented a vision of hope—faint though it may have been.

Just as neglecting God and justice had led to disaster, the prophets saw how returning to God and justice could restore the nation. God proclaimed through Amos, "Seek good and not evil, that you may live" (Amos 5:14). Faithfulness opens up new possibilities in the divine-human relationship. Jonah discovered that even evil Nineveh got a reprieve from divine judgment as a result of fasting, repentance, and changed behaviors.

The dynamic and interdependent realities of human and divine freedom motivate the prophetic imagination. We can change: We can restore the natural world, we can feed the hungry, the poor can find homes and good work, nations can promote the well-being of all their citizens, and the wealthy and powerful can be honest and generous.

Live the Story

In *The Powers That Be: Theology for a New Millennium*, theologian and Bible scholar Walter Wink's ground-breaking work on the political, economic, and powers that shape our values, behaviors, and allegiances, he asserts that

1) The "powers that be"—whether governments, corporations, or religious institutions—are essentially good, providing the framework necessary for creativity and order in our common lives.

2) These powers are fallen and often become agents of oppression, injustice, and violence.

3) These powers can be redeemed, enabling them to promote the common good through life-supporting forms of justice and order supportive of rich and poor alike.[7]

The prophets, as well as writers of New Testament texts such as Revelation, recognized that powers and principalities can be agents of violence and injustice. They also recognized the potential for governmental, religious, and economic institutions to become agents of creative transformation when their ultimate goals are justice and righteousness.

Corporate entities as well as individuals are called to live by an ethic of blessing, seeking the good of everyone whom their decisions affect, directly or indirectly. How have the powers that be had a positive influence on your life? How have they had a negative influence? How have they lived up to an ethic of blessing? How have they failed to live up to this standard?

The apostle Paul challenges us to not "be conformed to the patterns of this world" but to "be transformed by the renewing of [our] minds" (Romans 12:2). How can you and your congregation avoid complacency and become prophetic agents of justice and righteousness in your community and around the world? What injustices might you address so that justice will "roll down like waters, and righteousness like an ever-flowing stream" (Amos 5:24)?

1. From *http://www.americanrhetoric.com/speeches/mlkihaveadream.htm* (3-18-13).
2. From *http://mlk-kpp01.stanford.edu/index.php/resources/article/annotated_letter_from_birmingham* (3-18-13).
3. From *The Prophets*, Abraham Joshua Heschel, page 102.
4. From Heschel, *The Prophets*, page 3.
5. From Heschel, *The Prophets*, page 4.
6. From *What Does the Lord Require? The Old Testament Call to Social Witness*, Bruce Birch (Westminster: Philadelphia, 1995), page 62.
7. For more on Walter Wink's work on the spiritual dimensions of corporate entities, see Walter Wink, *The Powers That Be: Theology for a New Millenium* (New York: Three Rivers Press, 1999).

3.

Hosea: Divine Passion and Human Infidelity

Hosea

Claim Your Story

Have you seen the bumper sticker that says, "Prays well with others"? Have you ever seen the ones that say, "No Jesus, no peace. Know Jesus, know peace," or "The Bible says it. I believe it. And that settles it"?

Recent studies suggest that 30 percent of North Americans participate in multiple spiritualities. They may join Christian worship and social action with Buddhist meditation, traditional Chinese medicine, and Native American sweat lodges. However, not everyone finds interfaith cooperation and faith sharing helpful. In 2002, the Lutheran Church—Missouri Synod censored a pastor who participated in an interfaith prayer service—involving Jewish, Muslim, Hindu, and other Christian leaders—following the attacks on 9/11.[1] When Claremont School of Theology, a United Methodist seminary in California, added programs for Jewish and Muslim students, some groups within the church demanded that the school lose its denominational funding and affiliation. (The United Methodist Church temporarily suspended its affiliation with Claremont before fully reinstating the school.)

It is clear that Hosea has no tolerance for the Canaanite religions, and their worship of Baal. These religions were characteristic of the indigenous cultures who lived in the Promised Land before Israel arrived. The choice for Hosea is either Yahweh (God) or Baal worship. There was no "both-and," no creative synthesis of worshiping the one true God and another faith tradition. Hosea was clear that one must choose "either-or," faith or faithlessness, salvation or damnation, God or Baal.

As you ponder Hosea's story, his family challenges, and his critique of Israel's infidelity, consider the following questions: In the course of your spiritual journey, how have you benefited from encounters with people of other faith traditions? When have you participated in interfaith worship services or gatherings or in rituals (non-Christian weddings, Jewish high holy days, Shabbat or Passover Seders) or spiritual practices (yoga, meditation, energy work) from other religious traditions? What are your thoughts about the relationship of Christianity to non-Christian religions?

Enter the Bible Story

Hosea contains some of the Bible's loftiest poetry about God's love for humankind. It also contains some of the most difficult scriptural passages about relations with women. To appreciate Hosea, we must wrestle with the book in its entirety; but we must also remember its historical and sociological context. The Near East in the eighth century B.C. was patriarchal and paternalistic. Women were considered their husband's possessions and were expected to be passive and obedient. Children, until they reached adulthood, likewise, were considered property. Disobedient children and adulterous wives could be subject to the death penalty.

We don't need to affirm every Bible verse to affirm that Scripture is a source of wisdom and inspiration. Faithfulness to Scripture may require challenging certain passages that we deem racist, sexist, sexually outmoded, and violent. We can accept what Rabbi Abraham Joshua Heschel describes as the divine pathos, God's intimacy and passion for the world and the children of Israel, without affirming the most violent biblical passages. We must exercise humility when making judgments about Scripture. We must also recognize that, many decades from now, our ancestors may judge some of our attitudes as morally deficient.

We will address God's passion and fidelity toward a wayward people by considering the following: 1) Hosea's marriage to Gomer; 2) the relationship of covenant, infidelity, and ultimate concern; 3) the relationship between the God of Israel and the Canaanite religions; 4) knowing God; and 5) hope in a time of despair.

The Marriage of Hosea and Gomer

Often people speak of their spouses as being heaven-sent. But in Hosea's case, his relationship with his wife Gomer was a nightmare, even though God had chosen Gomer to be the prophet's wife, telling Hosea, "Go, marry a prostitute and have children of prostitution, for the people of the land commit great prostitution by deserting the LORD" (1:2). Hosea's marriage reflected God's painful and passionate love for this wayward people, whom God had chosen to be God's own. Through his own marital difficulties, Hosea gained insight into God's relationship with Israel; and he was able to preach words of judgment and grace to a nation that placed its hope in worshiping other gods.

In the Book of Hosea, God's anger burns brightly; but God's love is equally powerful in its reconciliation and healing. In the Book of Hosea, God vacillates between words of love and shouts of abuse. And Hosea's relationship with Gomer is not one that married couples should emulate: He is abusive and patriarchal, and she is unfaithful.

The language that Hosea uses with Gomer alternates between threat and reconciliation, and harassment and gentleness. This sort of language is characteristic of the abusive spouses who control their partners by following violent outbursts with promises of better days ahead. We cannot condone such relationships in the church nor can we advise battered spouses to stay in their marriages in obedience to God's plan for marriage. The One who came that we might have abundant life stands against abuse in all its forms.

As is the case of abusive marriages, the abuse also extends to the children; and we see this in the Book of Hosea. Hosea, at God's command, named his children "Jezreel" (which would be similar to someone in today's world naming a child "Hiroshima" or "Twin Towers"), "No compassion," and "Not my people." These names seem cold, even cruel, to us. But Hosea's contemporaries would have looked beyond the usual monikers and see the descriptions of God's justifiable anger toward Israel's infidelity. They would have recognized "Jezreel" as a reference to King Jehu of Judah's brutal massacre of the house of King Ahab of Israel years earlier in the Jezreel Valley on account of Ahab's idolatry.

God is passionate, even jealous, and will not share allegiance with any other being. Turning away from God leads to chaos, injustice, and destruction.

About the Christian Faith

Metaphors for God

Today, many people are sensitive to the language we use to describe God's nature and activity. No language can fully describe God, and all God-language is metaphorical. We use human words from our experience to describe God's nature. These words are intended to be comparative and figurative, not literal. Hosea, writing nearly 3,000 years ago, speaks of God as "husband" and "father." In Hosea's time, husbands controlled wives and fathers controlled sons. Adultery and disobedience were unforgivable behaviors. Theologians have sought both to critique and expand our metaphors for God to include feminine as well as masculine imagery. How would Hosea's narrative differ had it pertained to a wife's forgiveness of her unfaithful husband? How might the treatment of Gomer's infidelity have been different had Hosea been writing in a time where husbands and wives were considered equal partners? How does our understanding of this passage change when we consider that although God is a God of judgment, God is primarily a God of love and mercy?

Covenant, Infidelity, and Ultimate Concern

Although by the time of Hosea, Israel was separated into Northern (Israel) and Southern (Judah) Kingdoms, Hosea—in addressing the priests and nobles of the Northern Kingdom—asserted that God's covenant with all of Israel was still in effect (1:10-11). Even though the country was prosperous during Hosea's lifetime, Hosea reminded the people that their well-being depended upon God and that infidelity would lead to a day of reckoning. With the death of King Jeroboam II (786–746 B.C.), the country would be thrown into political and economic chaos, and Assyria would once again become a threat.

The Northern and Southern Kingdoms existed because God had made a covenant with the children of Israel. This was not a covenant of equals but the covenant of an all-powerful God with an oppressed people. God's continued covenant with the people required their faithfulness. These covenant people were set apart by their fidelity to the God who had called them and to the laws that God had established on Sinai to create a unique, justice-loving people. God's relationship with Israel can be summarized in the words of Deuteronomy 26:5-9:

> Then you should solemnly state before the LORD your God:
>
> "My father was a starving Aramean. He went down to Egypt, living as an immigrant there with few family members, but that is where he became a great nation, mighty and numerous. The Egyptians treated us terribly, oppressing us and forcing hard labor on us. So we cried out for help to the LORD, our ancestors' God. The LORD heard our call. God saw our misery, our trouble, and our oppression. The LORD brought us out of Egypt with a strong hand and an outstretched arm, with awesome power, and with signs and wonders. He brought us to this place and gave us this land—a land full of milk and honey."

God's relationship with Israel was both unilateral and dialogical. God chose this people, saved them from captivity, and gracefully led them through the wilderness. Drawing on the metaphor of a marriage, God is profoundly monogamous and expects fidelity from the chosen nation. God's commandment "You must have no other gods before me" (Exodus 20:3; Deuteronomy 5:7) is at the heart of God's covenant with Israel.

The famous twentieth-century theologian Paul Tillich believed that, despite protests to the contrary by atheists and agnostics, everyone has a "god." One's god is the ultimate concern or loyalty around which one shapes one's life. Our ultimate concern can be the One True God; or it can be something else: wealth, possessions, nationalism, comfort, recognition. Our ultimate concern is what is most important to us: the reality to which we give allegiance in return for fulfillment and wholeness.

Obviously, we have many concerns around which we shape our lives. For example, consider the question: If your house were burning, what would you risk your life to recover? Many of us would name family members, but we might also add photo albums or some other cherished possession. (While my first choice would be my multi-generational family, as a writer, I must confess that my next choice would be my computer!)

The problem with many of our ultimate concerns is that they simply aren't ultimate. They cannot deliver on their promises of fulfillment and security. We give them everything—our hearts, our time, and the sweat of our brow—only to find that they don't hold up. We put our faith in these false gods only to discover our lives are in shamble when the company downsizes, the stock market collapses, or our possessions can't cure cancer or a broken heart. This difference between God and all of the false gods that compete for our attention is at the heart of Hosea's message. Only God can be the peoples' ultimate concern. Their dalliances with foreign deities lead God's people on a path of destruction. In centering our lives on the Ultimate, we give allegiance and make sacrifices, and discover that God alone supports and saves us when all other concerns have left the stage, unmasked as idols and illusions.

Israel's God and the Canaanite Religions

Today, Christians practice yoga and Tai Chi, and go to acupuncturists and Buddhist retreat centers. They claim that their participation in other religious practices deepens their faith as Christians. While we don't know what Hosea would have thought about today's multiple spiritualities, we do know that he saw the children of Israel's participation in the practices of other religions as harmful not only to true worship but also to the Israel's political, economic, and spiritual health. Hosea abhorred any accommodation of Canaanite religion. He taught that one must follow either God or Baal—not both.

We don't know a great deal about the Canaanite religions, and much of what we know comes from prophetic writings such as Hosea (which aren't exactly impartial sources). It appears that Canaanite religions focused primarily on fertility in nature and human life. The sexual relationships of male and female gods renewed the earth, bringing spring rains to give life to plant, tree, and field after the frosty death of winter. Practitioners of the native religions worshiped at special places, often sacred trees, where they made sacrifices to ensure a good harvest. The prophets suggest that temple prostitution, which joined earth and heaven through sexual intercourse, was an essential part of the Canaanite religions. The story of Gomer and Hosea further suggests that ritual sexual activities were often employed by laypeople to promote fecundity in nature.

At any rate, Hosea was clear that an acceptance of Canaanite gods and traditions was a rejection of the God of Israel.

Knowing God

Hosea not only wants God's people to choose God over Baal, he wants them to truly know the One True God of Israel. According to God's message spoken through the prophet, "My people are destroyed from lack of knowledge" (4:6). Hosea is referring not to factual knowledge, but to relational knowledge: knowledge of our total dependence on God.

For Hosea, God's Law is not an external rule but an internal reality written on the heart. God's Law set apart the Hebrews as a people and created a community of justice and care. Turning away from God's Law not only leads to personal immorality but also to injustice. "Knowing God" means setting your life in alignment with God's vision for yourself, your community, and nation. It is the foundation for everything from economics to governance and foreign relations. Ignorance of God's ways can lead only to devastation in the family, community, nation, and non-human world.

Hosea's call for the nation to bring itself in line with God reminds us that even in a secular state, economics and politics become corrupt and destructive when people forget their spiritual and ethical values. Hosea's words raise the question: Where have we turned from our spiritual values to follow other gods? What are the "gods" that we serve instead of serving God? Are the realities of environmental distress, the growing division of rich and poor, and the political polarization of our time reflections of our failure to know God's vision for our lives? Hosea would answer with a resounding yes. He would note that the destruction of the earth and neglect of our most vulnerable citizens is related to our chasing after other gods.

Hope in a Time of Despair

Destruction is imminent for the Northern Kingdom. Their former alliance with Assyria, which included erecting a statue of the god Ashur in the Temple, will eventually lead to the collapse of the nation. Following the death of King Jeroboam II, political and economic despair seem inevitable and the people are hopeless. Their infidelity and immorality have separated them from God. Their only hope is divine reconciliation grounded in repentance and fidelity.

Hosea believes that God is a passionate God. What we do matters to God, bringing feelings of joy or suffering to God's heart. It pains God to see us go astray. God feels the suffering of the children of Israel and yearns for their return. Still, beyond despair there is hope; because God's love and mercy will heal the wounds we have caused one another and God.

Listen to these words as if they are addressed to you personally, to your community of faith, to your nation, and to the nations of the world:

> How can I give you up, Ephraim? . . . .
> My heart winces within me,
>   my compassion grows warm and tender.
> I won't act in the heat of my anger;
>   I won't return to destroy Ephraim;
> for I am God and not a human being,
>   the holy one in your midst. (Hosea 11:8-9)

God truly loves the world and God's people. The difference between God and humans is that God is ultimately graceful and forgiving.

Grace in the New Testament

Hosea's description of God's relationship with Israel (Ephraim) echoes in Jesus' parable of the prodigal son (Luke 15:11-32). Although the lost son has forfeited all rights as an heir by claiming his inheritance prematurely, his father welcomes him home, celebrating his return with a feast and signs of restoration to his place in the family. The apostle Paul affirms God's unmerited grace in his affirmation that "God shows his love for us, because while we were still sinners Christ died for us" (Romans 5:8).

Resurrection Awaits the Broken Nation

God will bring wholeness back to persons and nations despite their turning from God's way. This vision of God is embodied in Jesus' statements on the cross, "Father, forgive them, for they don't know what they're doing" (Luke 23:34). As Jesus wept over unfaithful and ignorant Jerusalem (Luke 19:41-44), perhaps these words of Hosea were in his thoughts:

> I will heal their faithlessness;
> I will love them freely,
> for my anger has turned from them.
> I will be like dew to Israel;
> he will blossom like the lily,
> he will cast out his roots
> like the forests of Lebanon. (14:4-5)

God's love of the people inspires a new heart within God's people reflected in the concluding words of the prophet:

> Truly, the LORD's ways are right,
> and the righteous will walk in them,
> but evildoers will stumble in them. (14:9)

Live the Story

Despite its challenges to the reader, the Book of Hosea is ultimately a message of hope. We can change. And in so doing, we open the doors to personal, congregational, and national transformation. Reconciliation can occur in Hosea's family and in God's relationship with Israel. New life can blossom again. Today, many people are hopeless as they look at global and national issues related to the environment, economics, and human rights. Others worry about their own futures as they face seemingly unsolvable problems. Hosea recognizes life in all its complexity, pain, and beauty and has hope in God's love for humankind. Like Hosea, we can experience healing and reconciliation when we place our trust in God and claim God's promises.

Where do you feel despair? What challenges hope in your congregation and in the nation? What practices might you turn to in order to renew or deepen your relationship with God? What changes and new forms of faithfulness might your congregation need to embody to face the challenges of a world filled with political, economic, social, and environmental uncertainty?

1. From *http://www.christianitytoday.com/ct/2002/julyweb-only/7-29-31.0.html* (3-18-13).

4.

Joel: Repentance and Restoration

Joel

Claim Your Story

In legal settings, the term *act of God* often describes an unexpected natural event that no one could have foreseen or prevented. Accordingly, because human agents are not considered responsible for such events, certain legal contracts and obligations may be nullified or deferred to a later date. While insurance companies and governmental agencies seldom invoke theological reasons for their behavior, their use of the term *act of God* is grounded in biblical precedent. The biblical tradition does not see God as an external force, unconcerned with the unfolding of history and the non-human world. Rather, God is the intimate intelligence and energy behind nature and human life. God is constantly bringing forth new possibilities, ideas, and events into our lives and world.

Theologians have argued about the extent of God's power. They have debated whether God determines every event or whether there is free play and real freedom that can be attributed to humans and the natural world. Theologians and lay people have debated about the ultimate causes of natural disasters such as Hurricane Katrina: Did God cause Katrina either as an expression of God's will or punishment for human sinfulness; or was the hurricane somehow primarily an act of nature, independent of any divine intentionality? Is God present in natural processes but as one of many causes? Are natural disasters wake-up calls to get our attention and call us to repentance?

According to a 2011 opinion poll by Public Religion Research Institute, 38 percent of Americans believe that God uses nature to bring judgment. When a tornado synchronously damaged a Evangelical Lutheran Church of America during a denominational meeting considering whether homosexuals can be considered for ordination, Baptist pastor John Piper asserted that the tornado was "a gentle but firm warning to the ELCA and all of us: Turn from the approval of sin. Turn from the promotion of behaviors that lead to destruction. Reaffirm the great Lutheran heritage of allegiance to the truth and authority of Scripture. Turn back from distorting the grace of God into sensuality."[2]

The relationship between God's actions and natural events is at the heart of Joel's message. Joel believes that a devastating plague of locusts comes from the hand of God. While Joel does not describe an exact one-to-one correspondence between God's actions and every event, he believes that God is the primary force behind this plague. Only repentance and heart-felt worship can change God's mind and thus avert complete disaster. The Book of Joel raises questions such as: Are natural events entirely the result of God's plan or punishment of human misdeeds? Can God change the direction of God's plans in response to our changed behavior? Is divine providence open ended or determined entirely in advance? Does God somehow depend on human behaviors in charting the course of divine activity? We will explore these essential theological questions in the course of reflecting on the theme of repentance and restoration in the Book of Joel.

Enter the Bible Story

A commercial describing the effect of unexpected events asserts. "Life comes at you fast!" Our world can turn upside-down in a moment by a few words from our physician, the impact of a funnel cloud, the collapsing of a levee, or a mechanical malfunction. As people in earthquake-prone California assert, "Shift happens!"

The prophet Joel reports the impact an event of biblical proportions on the people of Judah, the Southern Kingdom of Israel. The prophet asks the elders of the community, "Has anything like this ever happened in your days?" (1:2b) as he witnesses the catastrophic effect of swarm after swarm of locusts. Listen to Joel's graphic description of the plague that has overrun the nation:

> What the cutting locust left,
> the swarming locust has eaten.
> What the swarming locust left,
> the hopping locus has eaten.
> And what the hopping locust left,
> the devouring locust has eaten.
> (Joel 1:4-5)

There is no place to run and no place to hide as these six-legged insects destroy crops, devour trees, and even swarm in peoples' homes. You may remember Alfred Hitchcock's movie *The Birds* and shudder at the destructive powers of the non-human world. Joel's description of locusts' terrorizing humans by invading their homes dwarfs Hitchcock's vision of terror. In contrast to Hitchcock, though, Joel sees God's hand moving through this plague. Although the prophet does not specify the sins that have led to this catastrophic occurrence, he believes that only a change of heart, revealed in transformed behaviors and worship, will deliver the nation from total destruction.

In reflecting on the interplay of repentance and restoration in the scant 73 verses of Joel, we will consider the following themes: 1) Joel's understanding of acts of God; 2) the power of prayer and worship to change the world; 3) the nature of God's relationship to the world; 4) the tension between God's intimate care for us, that is, people who share our religious beliefs and heritage, and God's care for others; and 5) the source of hope in challenging times.

Joel's Understanding of Acts of God

It is no accident that the name *Joel* can be translated as "YHWH is God." The underlying theme of Joel's vision of the divine-human call and response is that 1) God is faithful, 2) God will right the wrongs the nation is suffering, and 3) God is ultimately in control of nature and human history. Joel knew the doctrines of omniscience (all-knowing), omnipresence (all-present), and omnipotence (all-powerful) first hand: God alone knows the human heart; God alone is present throughout the universe; and God alone determines the overall course of human life and the non-human world.

Today, as a result of more holistic understandings of health and illness, we now recognize that all illness is meaningful, whether socially, personally, spiritually, or theologically. Joel would have affirmed this sentiment both in relationship to human health and events in the natural world. The plague of locusts is not just a random and meaningless event. It reflects the impact of human behaviors on nature; but more important, it reveals God's will. According to Joel's vision of reality, God works in history and nature to bring about God's purposes. This can be spiritually consoling; but it can also be spiritually unsettling insofar as both evil and good must, either completely or partially, be attributed to God's action. It is no accident that popular Christian authors such as Rick Warren assert that every important event in our lives has been planned in advance by God without our consent or consultation. Warren unabashedly states that our family of origin, DNA, physical and mental abilities, successes, and traumas are "father-filtered" and bear the marks of divine intentionality. While Joel may not be as deterministic as John Calvin, who famously asserted that not a leaf falls without God's consent, he believes that natural disasters and international events reflect God's responses to individual, social, and political decisions. God punishes and rewards according to our actions. God can change God's attitude toward us, depending our responses to the events of our lives. God's mercy can intervene in the course of affairs, mitigating the effect of our infidelity and God's previous intentions to punish us.

Can Prayer Change God's Mind and Our Circumstances?

Joel sees history as the result of an ongoing divine-human call and response. In words repeated in Ash Wednesday liturgies, Joel's affirmation of God's creativity invites us to personal and social transformation.

> Yet even now, says the LORD,
> return to me with all your hearts,
> with fasting, with weeping,
> and with sorrow;
> tear your hearts
> and not your clothing.
> Return to the LORD, your God,
> for he is merciful and compassionate,
> very patient, full of faithful love,
> and ready to forgive. (Joel 2:12-13)

We cannot control God's actions, but we can hope that our changes bring changes in God's plans for the future. God knows what is going on in the world and has both the will and the ability to respond to changing circumstances.

> Who knows whether [God] will have a
> change of heart,
> and leave a blessing behind him. (2:14)

Joel does not give us a methodology for world-changing worship, but he affirms that worship and prayer must be heart-felt and reflected in our external behavior.

Does God Change?

One of my favorite hymns is "Great Is Thy Faithfulness":

> Great is thy faithfulness!
> Morning by morning new mercies I see.[3]

The lyrics praise God for providing all that we need, for pardoning our sins, for promising a lasting peace in our world, and for God's continual presence and guidance. Thomas O. Chisholm, who wrote the words to this hymn, drew inspiration from Lamentations 3:22-23:

> Certainly the faithful love
> of the LORD hasn't ended;
> certainly God's compassion isn't through!
> They are renewed every morning.
> Great is your faithfulness.

Joel, in his message of ultimate hope in a time of catastrophe, echoes these verses from Lamentations. Theologians for centuries have wrestled with the question, "Does God change?" One perspective says that God has determined every event that occurs from eternity and that all things, including salvation and damnation, flow from God's eternal decision. Another perspective says that God is constantly doing new things in our world. According to this view, God's providence, or care for human beings and all of creation, is open-ended and relational. What we do makes a difference to God and, in some ways, changes God's actions in the world.

Joel believes that God is active in determining the course of nature and human affairs and that God has the ability to change God's mind. Our hope rests, then, on an ever-faithful God, who responds in real time to prayer and repentance. When humans amend their behavior, reconciling with God, nature and society alike are transformed for the good.

Is God's Love Parochial or Universal?

On the first Christian Pentecost, which we celebrate as the birthday of the church, Peter cites Joel 2:28-32:

> After that I will pour out my spirit
> upon everyone;
> your sons and daughters will prophesy,
> your old men will dream dreams,
> and your young men will see visions.
> In those days, I will also pour out my
> spirit on the male and female slaves....
> But everyone who calls on the LORD's
> name will be saved. (2:28-29, 32a)

Peter quotes Joel to explain that God's revelation is universal, breaking down the barriers of age, language, gender, race, and ethnicity. Peter envisions a democracy of the spirit in which all people can experience God's inspiration. He interprets Joel having a universalist message, similar to that of the Book of Jonah. God cares for humans and non-humans, the children of Israel and foreigners. (See Jonah 3:1–4:11.)

But when we read Joel apart from the Christian lens of Peter's speech, it is not clear that the prophets message applies to all people. Joel may be referring to a restored nation of Israel, in which the people experience God's presence in their hearts instead of as a reality imposed from the outside.

Regardless of Joel's original intent, two things are clear: 1) in a restored nation of Israel, divisions caused by class, economics, age, and social standing will disappear; 2) people can experience God directly through dreams, prophetic words, and visions. Taking Joel seriously today can help us overcome today's divide between spirituality and institutional religion, reflected in the number of people who describe themselves as "spiritual, but not religious."

About the Christian Faith

The Nature of Providence and Election

Christians have debated the scope of God's love and salvation. Strict Calvinists believe that God determines in the beginning who will be saved and who will be damned. This idea, often described as "double predestination," takes salvation entirely out of our hands. It's all grace, provided you are one of the elect. For the lost, it is literally "damned if you do; damned if you don't." In contrast, the Arminian-Wesleyan tradition maintains the human and divine freedom to change. This viewpoint asserts that God calls all people but that we have the freedom to accept or reject God's call. The ultimate question, to quote a popular and controversial book by Rob Bell, is, "Does love win?" Does God eventually save everyone, or does our freedom place a limit on God's love?

The Source of Hope When Our World Has Collapsed

It is clear that the nation of Judah has been traumatized politically, economically, and ecologically. While Joel does not specifically mention military threats, other Old Testament texts describe Judah's precarious political and military situation. The once-great kingdom of David faces threats from Babylon and Assyria, Edom and Egypt. The economy has collapsed due to the devastation wrought by an invasion of locusts. Economic depression has devastated peoples' lives, shattered their dreams, and left them hopeless as they ponder the future. No doubt, many wonder if God has abandoned the nation altogether or, worse yet, that God is powerless to right the wrongs of history and restore the world.

In such a setting, God's ability to change the course of history provides a life-transforming image of hope. God proclaims a holy war, recruits a military force, and defeats Israel's enemies. Joel rejoices, "The LORD became passionate about this land, and had pity on his people. The LORD responded to the people" (2:18-19a). God restores the natural cycle of seedtime and harvest not just for humankind's sake but also out of care for the earth itself. Joel says:

> Don't fear, fertile land;
>> rejoice and be glad
>> for the LORD is
>>> about to do great things! (2:21)

Nation and nature alike are healed through God's passionate love. Freed from the devastation of human armies and natural disasters, Israel can in some future time live joyfully and faithfully because God "is a refuge for his people" (3:16). In the age to come, "Jerusalem will be holy, and never again will strangers pass through it" (3:17b). God will dwell in Zion, spiritually uplifting the people and making the earth fruitful:

> In that day
>> the mountains will drip sweet wine,
>> the hills will flow with milk,
>> and all the streambeds of Judah
>>> will flow with water;
>> a spring will come forth
>>> from the LORD's house
>>> and water the Shittim Valley. (Joel 3:18)

We don't know the exact date when Joel was written. Scholars guess that it could have been penned anywhere between the ninth and second centuries B.C. Likewise, for Joel's original audience, the date of Israel's restoration is uncertain. But it will happen, Joel declares, because God is faithful and loving and no human and natural force can thwart God's ultimate purpose for humankind and the historical process. God is always near!

Live the Story

Mother Teresa of Calcutta once stated that her goal was to do something beautiful for God. The implication of her statement is that what we do really matters to God. God hears our prayers, experiences our worship, and responds to our actions. Our actions can bring greater or lesser beauty to God's experience and can enhance or weaken God's influence in the world.

If our actions and worship really make a difference to God, and somehow shape God's experience and actions, what does this reality mean for your ethical behavior? How would you change your life if you truly believed Jesus' statement, "When you have done it for one of the least of these brothers and sisters, you have done it for me?" (Matthew 25:40). Since Joel is addressing nations and policy makers as well as individuals, how might this change our attitudes as citizens toward issues of economic justice, healthcare, and foreign policy? Where do you and your congregation need to "tear your hearts" (2:13), or show authentic repentance? Would a national day of fasting and repentance be an appropriate response to our current economic and social situations?

Joel challenges us to consider the relationship between our actions and God's presence in the world. What would it mean to put issues of justice and righteousness at the front of every political and economic decision? What would it mean to recognize that we are held morally accountable for the impact of our actions?

1. From http://www.christiancentury.org/article/2011-03/poll-most-americans-dont-blame-god-disasters (3-25-13).
2. From http://www.desiringgod.org/blog/posts/the-tornado-the-lutherans-and-homosexuality (3-25-13).
3. Taken from "Great Is Thy Faithfulness" © 1923, 1951 Hope Publishing Co., Carol Stream, IL 60188. Used by permission.

5.

Amos: Spirituality, Ethics, and Economics

Amos

Claim Your Story

A popular bumper sticker among evangelical Christians proclaims "Honk if you love Jesus." Another popular bumper sticker retorts, "If you love Jesus, seek justice. Any fool can honk."

While spirituality often involves solitary moments of prayer and meditation, our spiritual lives also take shape in our responsibilities as family members, friends, and citizens. The message of the prophets is that all religion has a public component related to culture, economics, political affairs, and the broader social environment.

The individual and social aspects of our faith sometimes find themselves in conflict. Is Christianity foremost about each individual's personal relationship with Jesus or about ushering in God's kingdom on earth? And are these two approaches to faith compatible?

In describing the social conditions of Harlem shortly after the turn of the twentieth century, Walter Rauschenbusch, a founder of the social gospel movement, noted, "Hell's Kitchen is not a safe place for saved souls." It isn't enough to give people the message of salvation if we don't also give them a glimpse of God's kingdom by meeting their basic needs and improving their situation. As James wrote, "Faith is dead when it doesn't result in faithful activity" (James 2:17). For the prophets, such faithful activity involved not only meeting needs as they arose but also insuring that social, political, and economic structures are just. Unjust social structures harm persons and create social ills that prevent millions of people from fulfilling their destiny as God's beloved children.

Amos connects worship with social and economic justice. He asserts that if one does not seek justice, one's worship will be futile and an insult to the Creator. Reading Amos invites us to consider the following questions: What is the relationship between individual and social morality? What role does political involvement play in one's faith? Can one be a Christian and be actively involved in economic and business relationships that directly harm persons and communities?

Enter the Bible Story

When a pastor named Steve preached about the importance of loving our neighbors, his parishioners responded with affirmation. They complimented him on his style and his practical advice for healthy family life and relationships at the office and school. But when Steve suggested that the congregation initiate a winter shelter program, housed in the church's gymnasium, and noted that there was a relationship between business practices that focused on financial gain at the expense of community life and the well-being of the most vulnerable members of the community, a number of members called for his resignation. This was Amos's problem as well. When he questioned whether the people of Israel had failed to live up to their call to be God's people and accused Israel of neglecting its poor, Amaziah, a priest representing the religious establishment, sought to silence the prophet: "Don't prophesy against Israel, and don't preach against the house of Isaac" (7:16). The job of religious leaders, Amaziah proclaimed, is to comfort the agitated, uphold the superiority of the nation, and support the interests of the wealthy and powerful, who provide the largesse necessary for the Temple's ministry. According to Amaziah, the vocation of priests and prophets is to mirror the nation's values, not to challenge them.

Amos indicts any faith perspective that uncritically ties God and nation or uncritically assumes that God is happy with the way things are. No doubt, the people of the Northern Kingdom of Israel perceived the herdsman and arborist from Tekoa, in the Southern Kingdom of Judah, as seditious.

We will explore Amos's understanding of the connection among ethics, economics, spirituality, and worship by considering the following issues: 1) the political and economic situation of eighth-century Israel, 2) the relationship between injustice and divine punishment, 3) the nature of authentic worship, 4) spirituality and justice-seeking, and 5) destruction and hope.

Amos was the earliest of the prophetic writers, writing in the eighth century B.C. during the reign of King Jeroboam II. Amos affirmed the relationships between faith, economics, and politics and made connections between injustice and economic inequality.

The Political and Economic Context

Under the leadership of Jeroboam II, the Northern Kingdom of Israel experienced prosperity that rivaled the fabled reigns of David and Solomon. With the Egyptians and Assyrians—the region's two superpowers—preoccupied with domestic issues and their immediate neighbors, Israel could reclaim lost territory and reassert its own sovereignty. The nation's political, business, and religious communities believed that God had truly blessed their nation. After a time of national insecurity, they were once again experiencing the benefits of being God's chosen people.

But not all was well. The body politic was not healthy: The gap between the rich and poor had widened; people of modest means had little access to the legal system; poverty led to heads of households selling themselves into virtual slavery to pay off debts; and farms were being foreclosed upon. Listen to Amos's indictment of the Northern Kingdom's economic policies:

> The Lord proclaims:
> For three crimes of Israel
>   and for four,
>   I won't hold back the punishment,
>   because they have sold the innocent
>   for silver
>   and those in need
>   for a pair of sandals.

> They crush the head of the poor
> into the dust of the earth,
> and push the afflicted
> out of the way. (Amos 2:6-7)

Sexual immorality was rampant; and some even used the money collected from fines and foreclosures to throw lascivious parties in the temple (2:7-8). Wealthy citizens gained their largesse by unfair labor practices. Among the sins of the wealthy power brokers, God is particularly offended by actions that involve crushing "the weak ... afflicting the righteous, taking money on the side, turning away the poor who seek help" (5:11, 12). Tax policy favored the wealthiest citizens. Speaking for God, Amos could barely restrain himself as he viewed houses built of ornate stone made from the proceeds from taxing and exploiting the weakest citizens (5:11).

Some people believe that history repeats itself and that the injustices Amos cites could easily describe the current economic situation in the United States and other nations, with growing income disparities. Amos would recognize that the recent global economic recession has hurt the poor more than the wealthy. He would ask why there is so much poverty in nations that have so much wealth. And he would be bothered by the number of people comfortable with the status quo and afraid to ask tough questions.

Human Injustice and Divine Punishment

The relationship between acts and consequences was central to Amos's understanding of history and divine-human relationships: injustice will eventually lead to destruction, while faithfulness to God leads to abundance. And we can see how our actions lead to destruction or abundance. Deforestation, for example, can cause soil erosion, reducing the amount of arable land in developing countries and exacerbating the problem of hunger. By contrast, canceling debts owed by developing nations, in the spirit of Leviticus 25, can lead to decreases in poverty and hunger and improvements in school and infrastructure.

Despite the prosperity of Israel's wealthiest citizens during Amos's career, Amos knew that destruction was lurking around the corner. And

About the Christian Faith and Across the Scripture

A Preferential Option for the Poor?

Amos criticizes the unjust practices of the wealthy and powerful. He sees God as a warrior siding with the concerns of the poor. The wealthy and powerful must sacrifice to ensure the well-being of the poor. And God will hold them accountable for any injustices they're guilty of. This same spirit is found in Mary's Song of Praise, known as the Magnificat (Luke 1:46-55): "With all my heart, I glorify the Lord....He has pulled the powerful down from their thrones and lifted up the lowly. He has filled the hungry with good things and sent the rich away empty-handed" (1:46, 52-53).

The words of Mary, Amos, and other biblical witnesses suggest that God has what some theologians refer to as "a preferential option for the poor." This does not mean that God loves the poor more than the wealthy but that God advocates for—and calls us to advocate for—the most vulnerable members of society. God wants abundant life for everyone, and the quest for abundant life requires profound shifts in our economic philosophy. Abundant life is more than giving people a meal or a place to sleep but ensuring that all of God's children can flourish economically, politically, and spiritually.

Israel's rich and famous would be held responsible for their callousness toward the rest of the population.

> Hear this word, you cows of Bashan,
>   who are on Mount Samaria,
>   who cheat the weak,
>   who crush the needy,
>   who say to their husbands,
>   "Bring drinks, so we can get drunk!"
> The LORD God has solemnly promised
>   by his holiness:
> The days are coming upon you
>   when they will take you away
>   with hooks. (Amos 4:1-2a)

Although God created the heavens and earth, God is also concerned with the minute details of business and politics. God hears the cries of the poor God abhors the ill-begotten comforts of those whose primary motive is profit, regardless of the consequences. "Doom to you who turn justice into poison, and throw righteousness to the ground!" (5:7).

Amos believes that God speaks through the natural world. Plagues and droughts are intended to be wake-up calls inviting us to return to the pathways of justice and compassion. In light of natural disasters, Amos urges the wealthy and powerful to "seek [God] and live" (5:4). True repentance embodied in compassionate for the nation's most vulnerable people may avert the catastrophe that awaits rich and poor alike.

Authentic Worship

Amos sees worship as a holistic enterprise involving not only singing hymns of praise but also business and political decisions, social values, and concern for the least of these. Worship is not primarily about feeling good, being intellectually stimulated, clapping our hands to the rhythm of a good praise band, or the sounds of a majestic organ. Even the best-crafted sermons are in vain if they aren't grounded in love for all of God's people. Worship is a whole-bodied experience intended to inspire us to transform the world by correcting injustice, being stewards of God's creation, ensuring the well-being of future generations, and restoring the fortunes of the impoverished and vulnerable. The world outside the temple or church is holy: We are to make the whole world our sanctuary in our quest for justice and beauty.

Amos is a liturgical killjoy. Imagine how the self-satisfied, patriotic worshipers felt when Amos delivered his words of judgment. No wonder the priest Amaziah wanted to get rid of this prophetic iconoclast.

Imagine how you would feel if a stranger were to stand up during a worship service and speak these words as though they came directly from God:

> I hate, I reject your festivals;
>   I don't enjoy your joyous assemblies....
> Take away the noise of your songs;
>   I won't listen to the melody of your harps.
> But let justice roll down like waters,
>   and righteousness
> like an ever-flowing stream. (5:21, 23-24)

Worship is an adventure of the spirit that compels us to reach out to the most vulnerable members of our communities. If the cries of the poor are drowned out by praise bands, organ preludes, and pontificating preachers, we will be unable to hear the voice of God in our hymns, Scriptures, and sacraments. Authentic worship challenges to us to lives of integrity and inspires us to encounter God in moments of despair as well as elation. Centuries after Amos, the Epistle of James reaffirmed the holistic nature of worship and spirituality with the words, "Faith is dead when it doesn't result in faithful activity.... As the lifeless body is dead, so faith without actions is dead" (James 2:17, 26).

The Relationship of Spirituality and Justice-Seeking

We have already touched on the phenomenon of people describing themselves as "spiritual but not religious," mostly out of a distrust for the church as an institution. They love the message of Jesus but see very little difference between the church and the culture at large. Amos would agree with such critiques but would challenge both insiders and outsiders to be both spiritual and religious. It's good to be religious by spending time in prayer, devotion, and worship; but we won't grow spiritually unless we also experience God in the least of these.

For the herdsman from Tekoa, there is no distinction between inner and outer, contemplation and action, worship and economics. Because of their apathy toward justice, the people will experience a spiritual famine:

They will wander from sea to sea,
 and from north to east;
they will roam all around,
 seeking the LORD's word,
 but they won't find it. (Amos 8:12)

Only a return to God's path of justice can satisfy our spiritual hungers and thirsts.

Destruction and Hope

A popular caricature of a prophet is the image of an eccentric person carrying a placard warning, "Repent, the end is near!" Amos, however, is ambivalent about the nation's future. Amos laments that Israel will be destroyed and that there will be little likelihood of national restoration. But Amos also repeats God's invitations, "Seek me and live" (5:4) and "Seek good and not evil, that you may live" (5:14). Amos twice pleads on behalf of the nation, begging to restrain God's wrath—"LORD God, please forgive!...LORD God, I beg you, stop!" the prophet pleads (7:2, 5). In both cases, God relents out of love for the people and in response to the prophet's faithfulness.

The future of the Kingdom of Israel is in doubt. It has sown injustice and violence and will reap what it has sown in national destruction. Assyria will soon overrun its gates, murder its leaders, and take the remaining into captivity. As he prepares to return to his herds and sycamores, Amos receives one last message from God. Humanity and nature will be restored. A holy people, set apart by God's grace and their just actions will emerge out of the rubble. The God of humans and non-humans will resurrect a new earth:

> The days are surely coming,
>   says the LORD....
> The mountains will drip wine,
>   and all the hills will flow with it.
> I will improve the circumstances
>   of my people Israel;
>   they will rebuild the ruined cities
>   and inhabit them.
> They will plant vineyards
>   and drink their wine;
> and they will make gardens
>   and eat their fruit.
> I will plant them upon their land,
>   and they will never again be plucked up
> out of the land
>   that I have given them. (Amos 9:13-15)

God's love is more enduring than God's punishment. God will restore the nation God "loved so deeply of all the families of the earth" (3:2). This generation will never again experience national sovereignty; but its descendants will seek good, act justly, and rejoice in God's gracefulness.

Live the Story

As you ponder Amos' message for today, imagine your own pastor or a layperson in your congregation or community being called to a prophetic ministry. How would your congregation receive a challenging prophetic message? What is your congregation's comfort zone for politics in the pulpit? What social messages would the congregation receive with affirmation and applause?

Amos believes that we cannot separate politics and religion. What issues do you think might be off limits in your congregation? In the past, some churches considered issues such as slavery and equal rights for women off-limits. Are there issues we're avoiding today that we'll some-day regret not talking about?

Once we broach these touchy subjects, we must consider how we talk about them. Christians have diverse perspectives on economic, political, and social issues. How do we know which perspective is most in line with God's will? We can't always know for sure, but we have plenty of guidance. Amos' message, and the witness of other prophets, teaches us that God has a preferential option for the poor and commands us to seek justice even if we don't always agree about how to do so. A commitment to justice is not optional but essential.

6.

Obadiah: Justice, Punishment, and Hope

Obadiah

Claim Your Story

On April 2, 2006, Charles Roberts entered an Old Order Amish schoolhouse in Nickel Mines, near my home in Lancaster, Pennsylvania. Before the morning ended, Roberts had shot ten young girls, killing five of them, before committing suicide. Our community was stunned and outraged by this unprovoked violence. But more stunning was the Amish community's response to this tragic event: They did not respond with vengeance or hatred. One of the survivors recalled one of her murdered classmates telling her classmates, "We must not think evil of this man." A local Amish farmer added, "He had a mother and a wife and a soul and now he's standing before a just God." The Amish community reached out in forgiveness and set up a fund to support his family.

The Book of Obadiah raises a variety of questions about how we should respond to acts of violence done against us and against people we love? Will God punish perpetrators of evil? Does God punish nations for their acts of oppression and injustice? Do people and nations receive a punishment proportional to what they have done? Although it is the shortest and one of the most overlooked books in the Old Testament, Obadiah is a treasure chest of big theological and ethical questions.

Enter the Bible Story

Following the death of Osama bin Laden, the leader of al-Qaeda and mastermind of the 9/11 attacks on the United States, President Barack Obama declared, "Justice has been done." We often hear law enforcement officers promise to "bring to justice" perpetrators of serious crimes. Although prosecution cannot undo the pain experienced by victims of crime, the criminal justice system provides a sense of closure that often helps people rebuild their lives.

The quest for justice has many forms, but all of them share a basic belief that there is a moral order in the universe and human life that is revealed in fairness and reciprocity of benefits and punishments. Our culture's notion of justice includes ideas such as a good day's work deserves fair compensation and punishment should fit the crime.

The Book of Obadiah is a testament to divine justice and asserts that evildoers must be punished for their infractions as part of the healing process. Obadiah's vision is rooted in Hebraic law, which proclaims, "You will give a life for a life, an eye for an eye, a tooth for tooth, a hand for a hand, a foot for a foot, a burn for a burn, a bruise for a bruise, a wound for a wound" (Exodus 21:23-25, see also Deuteronomy 19:21). This principle, known by the Latin term *lex talionis* (meaning "law of retaliation"), seems cold on its surface. But its initial purpose was not only to ensure strict punishments but also to limit retaliation. It says that the severity of the punishment must not exceed the severity of the crime. A tribe, community, or nation must not launch unlimited retaliation for a finite crime. If a member of the tribe is killed by someone from a rival tribe, this principle limits retaliation to a single life. It allows the tribe to kill the guilty party; it does not allow the tribe to wipe out the guilty party's village.

Obadiah's vision of the relationship of divine justice and human hope requires us to consider the following themes: 1) the authorship and context of Obadiah; 2) Edom's violation of divine justice; 3) Obadiah's concept of divine justice, especially as it is meted out to the people of Edom; 4) the day of Yahweh and the judgment of the nations; and 5) divine justice as a source of hope for Israel and ourselves.

Authorship and Context

No one is certain when Obadiah was written, nor do we know much about its author. The name *Obadiah*, "servant of God," appears several times in the Old Testament; but none of the individuals to whom it refers can be connected with certainty to the author of the text. Obadiah was written early in the sixth century B.C. or later, because it deals with the role that the nation of Edom had played in the Babylonian invasion of Judah. Babylon conquered Judah in 587 B.C.

Obadiah is clear that God controls history in terms of victory and defeat, reward and punishment. God's justice will be done eventually, and Jerusalem's former glory will be restored.

Edom's Violation of Divine Justice

One of the first questions people often have when they read Obadiah is: "Why is God picking on Edom? Why must Edom be destroyed?" According to the Hebrew tradition, Judah and Edom are descendants of Isaac's twin sons, Jacob and Esau, respectively. So the two nations were joined by a common heritage. This fraternal relationship suffered when Edom refused to defend Judah during the Babylonian siege. Obadiah says that, worse yet, Edom did violence to Judah's vanquished citizens:

> You should have taken no pleasure
> over my brother
> on the day of my misery....
> You shouldn't have entered
> the gate of my people
> on the day of their defeat; ...
> you shouldn't have stolen his possessions
> on the day of his distress.
> You shouldn't have waited on the roads
> to destroy his escapees;
> you shouldn't have handed over his survivors
> on the day of defeat.
> (Obadiah 12a, 13a, c-14)

Edom betrayed Judah and violated its relationship with God. Although Edom may have initially been motivated by security concerns, its self-interest turned to violence and greed as it joined the marauding Babylonian armies in plundering Jerusalem. Now, Obadiah says, Edom must pay in full. Its mountain hideaways and fortresses will prove useless to protect it from God's wrath.

You Get What You Deserve: God's Punishment of Edom

Obadiah believes that we live in an orderly universe in which people and nations are punished for the wrongs they have done to others. Obadiah exemplifies the Hebraic belief that there is a relationship of acts and consequences in terms of God's personal ordering of history. Goodness will always be rewarded, while evil eventually leads to punishment—not in some future lifetime but in this life. Deuteronomy 28:1 proclaims, "Now if you really obey the LORD your God's voice, by carefully keeping all his commandments ... then the LORD your God will set you high above all the nations on earth." In contrast, those who disobey God's Law will be cursed, defeated, and/or afflicted with illness, failure, and poverty (Deuteronomy 28:15-68).

Obadiah recognizes that the Southern Kingdom of Judah's sin has led to the nation's destruction. God meted out this punishment through invaders from Babylon and perhaps even Edom. But Babylon and Edom will be punished for their hand in Judah's destruction. Edom will be laid waste, annihilated, and sold into captivity in the same manner as it had treated its brother Jacob.

While this approach to rewards and punishment enables victims of crime and oppression to feel as though justice has been done when criminals and oppressors are punished, it leads to a crisis of faith when criminals and oppressors appear to prosper. Disease and destruction lead to a theological crisis when seemingly good people die of cancer and suffer affliction and reprobates live long and affluent lives. Such an issue of unjust suffering emerges when God's chosen nation, Israel, is humiliated and defeated while its enemies seem to get off without consequences.

The Book of Job tackles the issue of unfair suffering on an individual level. When Job, the most blameless of humans, loses family, wealth, and health, he has to reject his acts-consequences understanding of rewards and punishments. Obadiah, in contrast, remains hopeful that Edom and other hostile nations will get their due. Hans Walter Wolff notes in his commentary on Obadiah, "In the dimmest of days, the words of Obadiah underline the unbelievable truth that God's hand can change everything." Obadiah rests his hope on God's ultimate punishment of Edom and God's ultimate restoration of Jerusalem. This hope in the unseen enables Obadiah to maintain his faith that God is ultimately in charge of history.

The Day of Yahweh, the Day of the Lord

Obadiah, like the other prophets, believes that God is near and that judgment can come at any moment. Amos proclaims, "Why do you want the day of the LORD? It is darkness not light" (Amos 5:18b). Obadiah echoes this idea that all will be judged by their works and that the majority of nations will receive punishment rather than reward. "The day of the LORD is against all the nations. As you have done, so it will be done to you; your actions will make you suffer!" (Obadiah, verse 15). The God who inspired nations to initiate a holy war against Edom will weigh every nation by the scale of justice and all will come up short.

One could use the Book of Obadiah to justify war as something ordained by God: "We have heard a message from the LORD—a messenger has been sent among the nations: 'Rise up! Let us rise against her for battle!'" (verse 1b). One could also use Obadiah's words to make the case (as discussed above) that God punishes nations for their immorality. While we are rightly appalled when people today suggest that natural disasters and terrorist attacks are God's will—punishment for a people's misdeeds—such suggestions have origins in Scripture.

Retribution and Restoration

Obadiah ends with a message of hope. A remnant of Judah will survive following the Day of the Lord. Jerusalem will be restored by God's actions in history, and the nation will regain some of its former greatness. More important, the restored nation will be faithful to God. Zion will be holy and its holiness will enable it to destroy its former oppressors, secure the former borders of the land, and once again live under God's leadership (verse 21).

Edom will perish and Judah will prosper. The people of Judah will return home, their nation will be revived, and justice will be done to their oppressors. It's hard to tell which is more satisfying to Obadiah: the restoration of Judah or the destruction of Edom.

Across the Scriptures

Punishing the Enemy

Obadiah is clear that Edom will get what it deserves at the hands of a righteous God. In the Sermon on the Mount, Jesus took another approach. While he didn't deny the realities of cause and effect or of personal responsibility, he taught his followers to "love your enemies and pray for those who harass you" (Matthew 5:44). He also told us not to wage holy wars against our enemies. "You have heard that it was said, *An eye for an eye and a tooth for a tooth*. But I say to you that you must not oppose those who want to hurt you. If people slap you on your right cheek, you must turn the left cheek to them as well" (Matthew 5:38). I suspect that Jesus' words inspired the Amish to forgive the perpetrator of the Nickel Mines massacre.

Live the Story

Obadiah's words can be used to justify terrorist acts, the eradication of native peoples, and the elimination of anyone who stands in the way of our perception of God's will.

Looking at the story from another perspective, how might Edom have justified its treatment of Judah? Edom might have rationalized that Judah was getting only what it deserved. Didn't Jacob trick our ancestor Esau out of the most fertile territory? Perhaps, their version of eye for an eye and sowing and reaping enabled them to rationalize their betrayal of Judah. They might have seen themselves as God's instruments of justice against a nation whose father had betrayed their ancestors.

It is challenging to see one's nation from another nation's perspective. When we see people in other nations holding signs that say, "Death to America," we are angry and have difficulty understanding why they hate us. We believe that we've done nothing to incur such animosity. Still, as a form of national confession, we also need to consider the impact of our foreign policy, often motivated by national self-interest, on others' attitudes toward us.

In light of the Amish response to the Nickel Mines tragedies, is it possible for us to forgive our nation's adversaries? How can we balance forgiveness for people who have perpetrated violence with national security and protection of our families? Can we forgive the sexual predator while ensuring that he or she receives appropriate incarceration and, after serving her or his sentence, supervision in church so that he or she can no longer hurt others? These are difficult questions that invite us to consider the relationship between personal forgiveness and institutional justice.

7.

Jonah: When Grace Goes Beyond Justice

Jonah

Claim Your Story

Theology matters. What we believe can change our behaviors and expectations. Susan knocked on the door of my study with tears in her eyes. She had just been in a conversation with her cousin, who stated that, without a shadow of doubt, Susan's deceased parents were condemned to hell because they had questions about the nature of the Trinity, the creation stories, and the virgin birth of Jesus. Susan confided, "My mother and father were good Christians, but they always asked questions and never accepted anything just because the preacher said it or it was found in Scripture." Susan's cousin had theological viewpoint that had no room for doubt and questioning, and her viewpoint led to a rift in her relationship with Susan.

That same week in May 2011, the followers of radio evangelist Harold Camping were devastated when his prediction of the Second Coming proved inaccurate. In expectation of the end of the world, many of his followers quit their jobs and sold their homes. Their theology left them homeless, bankrupt, and disillusioned. It is evident that our theology makes a difference and can shape how we view issues of contraception and abortion, the age of the earth and the theory of evolution, and persons of other faiths.

To many people, Jonah is simply a fish story, irrelevant to modern people. But when we get beyond this humorous tale about a reluctant prophet, we discover that Jonah is among the most theologically provoca-tive books in the Old Testament. Jonah appropriately follows Obadiah among the books of minor prophets. The prophetic figures Jonah and Obadiah have a similar theology. Both believe that divine justice is inexorable and unswerving. According to the respective prophets, Nineveh (in Jonah), like Edom (in Obadiah), deserves to be leveled. If God doesn't punish Nineveh by destroying the city, the whole moral order of the universe collapses. Jonah cannot believe in a moral order that includes mercy for his enemies and oppressors.

As you read the Book of Jonah, consider your own attitudes toward people who have hurt you or our nation. Following the 9/11 attacks, I recall a conversation with a colleague in my department. This otherwise anti-war professor blurted out, "Why don't we just nuke the terrorists?"

Deep down, whom do you wish to "nuke"? What actions might pro-voke you to favor merciless retribution? Which opponents of our nation are you guilty of dehumanizing? Can we be graceful toward people and nations who wish to harm us? These are not academic questions but have an impact on our interpersonal and international relations.

Enter the Bible Story

Jonah is a theological masterpiece, a parable that turns upside-down the prophet and his people's understanding of the relationship of God's justice and mercy. On its surface, Jonah is the story of a reluctant prophet and a cautionary tale about what happens when we don't follow God's call in our lives. But when we look a little deeper, we find a story about a prophet who believes that he understands God's will and is incredulous when God corrects his understanding of divine justice. Like Obadiah, Jonah holds to the orthodox Hebraic view of justice: an eye for an eye and a tooth for a tooth. In his mind, Nineveh deserves to be leveled, and God should destroy it. Anything less would be unjust. But God asks Jonah to step beyond what he knows and to be obedient to God's vision for a particular time and place. This is more than Jonah can take. So he flees to Tarshish, which may have been near the Strait of Gibraltar—the farthest point in the known world for people in the Ancient Near East.

We will explore the issue of this parable of grace and justice by considering the following: 1) the authorship and context of the Book of Jonah, 2) Jonah's strange journey, 3) God's presence and activity in the human and non-human world, 4) the piety of pagans, and 5) Jonah's contribution to theological reflection.

The Authorship and Context of Jonah

As is true of so many other ancient texts, the authorship of Jonah is a mystery. The story is told in the third person, describing the misadventures of the only biblical prophet called specifically to preach to a foreign land. Some scholars believe that the central figure of the story, Jonah, is patterned after an earlier "Jonah," the Son of Amittai, a prophet who called for the recovery of lost territory during the time of the morally ambiguous Jeroboam II (785–745 B.C.).

The date of the Book of Jonah is also unknown, although most scholars assume that it was penned at some point after Assyria's annihilation of the Northern Kingdom of Israel in 724 B.C. Scholars have dated Jonah as early as the seventh century B.C. and as late as the third century B.C.

A number of scholars see Jonah as a *midrash*, or elaborative explanation, of Jeremiah 18:8: "If that nation I warned turns from its evil, then I'll relent and not carry out the harm I intended for it." The parable of the reluctant prophet, no doubt representative of the Jewish people, challenges parochial images of God's mercy and invites readers to see God's love as universal, embracing even the oppressor and enemy.

Jonah's Strange Journey

Virtually every Sunday school child learns the tale of Jonah. For years, Assyria, the homeland of the city of Nineveh, had threatened the peace of the Northern and Southern Kingdoms, Israel and Judah, until it finally destroyed the Northern Kingdom, humiliating its leaders and pillaging its cities. As the story goes, "once upon a time," a prophet is called to travel to preach doom and gloom to the evil empire. To Jonah, Nineveh's immorality rivals that of the notorious ancient cities of Sodom and Gomorrah. Jonah believes that the city deserves to be destroyed, and that is exactly his message. But he doesn't want to be the one to tell the Ninevites that destruction is on the way. So he secures a place on ship headed to the edges of the known world and tries to do what he knows is impossible: flee from God's awareness and activity.

God sends a storm that threatens to destroy the ship. The sailors cast lots to determine who is responsible for this calamity, and the lots point to Jonah. Jonah fesses up to fleeing from God and asks his shipmates to throw him overboard to appease the Lord. God sends a large fish to swallow Jonah, saving the prophet's life and providing him lodging for three days. Jonah sings a psalm from the belly of the whale, thanking God for God's deliverance and mercy. Although Jonah does not repent his disobedience, he journeys to Nineveh and walks throughout city, proclaiming its imminent destruction.

Across the Scriptures

The Sign of Jonah

In Matthew 12:38-41 and Luke 11:29-32, Jesus speaks of the "sign of Jonah"—the threat of destruction—as the only sign his hard-hearted contemporaries will receive. Jesus compares his call to repentance to Jonah's message to Nineveh. The Son of Man challenges people to repent, to change their ways and live in expectation of God's coming reign. Matthew's Gospel connects Jonah's three days in the belly of a great fish with the three days from Good Friday to Easter Morning.

Something amazing happens. From the greatest to the least, from king to cattle, the entire city of Nineveh repents and institutes a fast, hoping to escape judgment. God responds by changing God's mind and saves the city. Jonah isn't pleased. From hilltop from which Jonah had hoped to see Nineveh annihilated, Jonah complains to God, objecting to God's mercy. God gives Jonah a shade plant to shield him from the day's heat, but the next day a worm kills the plant. Jonah cries out in anguish, wishing that he would die. He no longer has the comfort of the plant's shade; and worse yet, his vision of an orderly universe of rewards and punishments has collapsed as a result of God's infinite mercy. The story ends with a question for Jonah and us: If you mourn the death of shade plant, may not I, God, feel sorry for the destruction of a great city and its inhabitants, both human and non-human?

We don't know how Jonah responded to that question.

God's Omnipresence

There is a popular saying: "You can run but you can't hide." Psalm 139 tells us that there is no place outside of God's care. If we descend to the depths of life, God is with us. If ascend to heights of joy, God is our companion. Even if we cover ourselves in darkness—depression, grief, and disobedience—our darkness is still light to God. When we attempt to escape from God, as Jonah did, we end up fleeing into the arms of the One who challenges, inspires, and loves us.

Jonah's God is omnipresent, omniscient, and omni-active. The idea of a deity who operates from outside the world, only occasionally intervening in world affairs, is foreign to Jonah. God is embedded in the challenges and ambiguities of our lives and of world affairs. God moves through nature in storm, plant, and fish. God moves through the human heart, calling for repentance. God knows Jonah's footsteps and travel plans; and God knows the evil of the Ninevites and hopes for their unexpected repentance. God is present in every event and seeks justice and healing of all creation and every person. While God demonstrates grace by forgiving Nineveh and giving Jonah a second chance, God's work in nature reflects God's dynamic power and untamed energy. Storm and sea monster also reflect God's providential care; they are frightening in their power yet ultimately intended to save humans and non-humans alike.

Pious Pagans

While much of Scripture, including Joel and Obadiah, takes a dim view of Israel's neighbors, the Book of Jonah recognizes the goodness of other ethnic groups. When the ship is in danger, the mariners cry out to their respective gods. The ship's captain wakens Jonah to call out to his own god, hoping and praying that Jonah's god will deliver the ship from disaster. Even after casting lots to discern the guilty party, the mariners do not want to sacrifice Jonah's life to calm the storm. Jonah must force his pagan shipmates to throw him overboard. When the storm subsides, the pagan mariners are filled with awe; give thanks to the God of Israel; and make vows, perhaps, to pursue a better life and be respectful of God's chosen people.

Despite their unspecified evil behavior, the citizens of Nineveh respond to God's call to repentance. Whereas, Jonah simply cries out words of doom and gloom, with no expectation that they will repent, the people put on sackcloth and ashes, turn from evil and violence, and proclaim a fast in hope that God will change God's mind. Even domestic animals participate in acts of repentance. The Book of Jonah asserts that God's love and mercy are universal and open to all nations.

Jonah as a Theological Masterpiece

Storytelling can sometimes be more life transforming that of abstract theological reflection. Think a moment of the books that have changed your life and opened you up to new images of God. No doubt, many of them were stories: *Joshua*, by Joseph Girzone; *The Shack*, by William Young; *The Screwtape Letters* and *Chronicles of Narnia*, by C.S. Lewis; *A Wrinkle in Time*, by Madeleine L'Engle; *The Prophet*, by Kahlil Gibran; *Pilgrim's Progress*, by John Bunyan; or *The Metaphor Maker*, by Patricia Adams Farmer. Jonah is just such a book. Like Job, Jonah is the story of "everyman" or "everywoman" as he or she seeks to fathom God's nature and work in the world.

Jonah's attempt to flee from God was not simply an act of defiance. He was also trying to stay faithful to what he knew to be true. Old Testament scholar Terence Fretheim notes, "Jonah does not flee because of unbelief or an absence of faith. Rather, he decides to flee because of a certain type of belief he has." Fretheim continues, "Jonah's problem is that God is being too lenient toward those who are guilty, more precisely, toward those whose guilt is so overwhelming that it would be unjust to let them go scot free."[1] Jonah, whose theological world was grounded in a rationally-ordered universe of linear and unbending reward and punishment, can't imagine living in a world where punishment is not executed on wrongdoers. God, in Jonah's view, cannot play dice with morality but must conform to strict laws of justice and retribution.

Jonah believes that he has every reason to be angry with God for forgiving the Ninevites. Miguel de la Torre, nineteenth-century Spanish general and governor of Puerto Rico, captures the dynamic that oppressed people face when they are asked or seek to reconcile with those who have harmed them: "How can we relate to those who bring subjugation, misery, and death to our people, our loved ones, and ourselves?"[2] Yet forgiveness is the only way for the oppressed to avoid becoming oppressors themselves. This was the message of Mahatma Gandhi, Martin Luther King, Desmond Tutu, and Nelson Mandela. Still, this is not intended to be what Dietrich Bonhoeffer described as "cheap grace," forgiving without acknowledging the pain you've experienced or accepting forgiveness without amending your behavior and lifestyle. Nineveh repented and God responded. Could it be that in the non-existent Chapter 5 (use your imagination!) of this "once upon a time story," Nineveh chose to turn from its expansionist international policy, rebuild nations it destroyed, and set up fair trade policies?

Jonah's vision of God's mercy invites us to consider the place of orthodoxy, or right belief. One of the main reasons to determine orthodoxy is to determine heterodoxy, or incorrect belief. Throughout Christian history, people have been persecuted, martyred, and executed because they were considered heretical. Of course, one person's orthodoxy is often another's heresy. During the Great Schism of 1054, which divided the church in the west (now the Roman Catholic Church) from the church in the east (now the Orthodox Church), leaders from both sides excommunicated one another. Centuries later, Roman Catholics considered reformers such as Jan Hus and Martin Luther as heretics. At the same time, Reformers saw the Roman Catholic Church as deviating from the biblical message. Among Protestants, Calvinists and Arminians disagreed on right belief when it came to the idea of election, with Calvinists insisting that God had predetermined whom God would save and Arminians (including John Wesley and his followers) arguing that salvation is conditional and depends on a person's response to God's grace. Christians today continue to debate correct belief, particularly with regard Christian theology's relationship to science and politics.

The orthodox Jonah is stunned by the possibility that God could be different than he had imagined. First, Jonah was shocked by the possibility that God's mercy and grace extended to all people, including the citizens of Nineveh. God's love even includes the non-human world. Second, Jonah could not fathom a God whose primary characteristic is mercy. Third, Jonah was amazed that God's mind could be changed. A living God can change course and do new things in response to changing conditions.

About the Christian Faith

Jonah as an Ecological Treatise

The Book of Jonah has long been a favorite of animal lovers. In Jonah, God's mercy extends not only to the people of Nineveh but to the animals as well. God communicates to a great fish, leaving the reader to ponder the nature of non-human intelligence and God's relationship with the animal world. The Book of Jonah continues the creation-affirming theology of Genesis 1:1-2:4 and Psalm 148–150, in which human and non-human alike are affirmed as reflections of God's wise creativity, able to respond to God's voice.

Can non-humans be instruments of God's grace? Do non-humans experience eternal life? Jesus claims that God cares for the birds of the air and lilies of the field (Matthew 6:25-34). The apostle Paul speaks of creation groaning and being drawn toward the same glory that God has in store for us (Romans 8:18-25). The non-human world matters to God. While we have a unique relationship with God, God's touches all creation with inspiration and love, and invites us to be planetary stewards.

Jonah presents a new kind of orthodoxy that challenges the linear cause-and-effect worldview outlined in Deuteronomy 28 and in the oracles of Obadiah. This is good news for Israel and us. Despite our erring ways,

God does not abandon us but seeks to awaken us to the grace in which we stand. At the end of the day, God's grace overcomes our sin and enables us to begin again.

Live the Story

Jonah raises some of the same questions as Obadiah but from the perspective of unmerited grace that allows God to embrace oppressors, evildoers, and garden-variety sinners, giving us much more than we deserve. Reading Jonah may bring to mind the words of John Newton's "Amazing Grace":

> Amazing grace! How sweet the sound
> that saved a wretch like me!
> I once was lost, but now am found;
> was blind, but now I see.

Grace may not free us entirely from the effects of our decisions. But grace liberates us to make new decisions that are healthier and more supportive of others. As we read Jonah, we have to remember that this story describes God's relationship with nations and was, no doubt, addressed to the nation of Israel as well as to individuals. Can we relate this message of mercy and forgiveness to international affairs today? What would it mean for our nation to be graceful to a nation or group that has harmed us? Can we balance justice with mercy in foreign affairs? If so, what would this look like in terms of national policy? Further, if nations can repent of their misdeeds, for what things should our nation repent? Where has our nation practiced injustice, violence, or immorality—whether politically, militarily, economically, or culturally? What would it mean to repent for our nation's misdeeds?

1. Terence Fretheim, *The Message of Jonah: A Theological Commentary* (Minneapolis: Augsburg/Fortress, 1977), pages 19, 33.
2. Miguel de la Torre, *Liberating Jonah: Forming an Ethic of Reconciliation* (Maryknoll, New York, 2007), page 1.

8.

The Prophetic Challenge Today

Hosea—Jonah

Claim Your Story

When my first grandson was just over a year old, he discovered the power of a mirror to shape his self-understanding. For months prior to that time, he had noticed the mirror in the first floor hallway almost every day as one of us carried him downstairs. He enjoyed the shapes and colors in the mirror and reveled in the fact that they were constantly changing. But one day, it dawned on him that the shapes in the mirror belonged to him and "Gabby" (his name for Grandpa Bruce). He had a look of surprise and then a smile of recognition as the figures in the mirror reflected our movements. Although he didn't have words for it at the moment, I could see that inside he was celebrating. "Hey, that's me in the mirror!"

Mirrors are often flattering. But some of us have discovered that looking in a mirror can be disturbing. "Who is that somewhat overweight, slightly balding person?" we may ask ourselves, and then sheepishly answer our own question, "Hey, that's me in the mirror."

The prophetic writings—and Scripture as a whole—hold up a mirror to our lives and communities. Sometimes what we see comforts us; but other times, we are disturbed when we recognize ourselves in the words of the prophets. We recognize our consumerism and prejudice, and we discover the relationship between our comforts and other peoples' poverty. In a manner similar to John the Baptist and, more recently, the revival preachers of my childhood, the prophetic writings present us, first, with bad news, showing us our failure and the failure of our institutions to live up to God's vision for our lives. Then they open the door to a new possibility, showing us the good news of God's love for humankind reflected in God's words of challenge and comfort. We are not condemned to repeat our sins over and over but can repent of our sinfulness and begin a new life and, as the apostle Paul says, we can become a "new creation."

In this final chapter, we will consider the relevance of the prophetic writings, discussed in this study, to our personal and corporate lives. To prepare, take time to reflect on the following questions, based on the first seven chapters of this text: Where have the prophetic writings challenged my priorities and lifestyle? In what ways have they challenged the values and practices of my congregation? What changes would I have to make to be faithful to the prophetic message for our time? What changes would my community and nation need to make?

Enter the Bible Story

The prophets experienced and shared God's message first hand. They presented an alternative, God's-eye view of the human condition that challenged socially accepted, yet unjust and unfaithful, religious and political practices.

It has been said that we need to have the Bible in one hand and the newspaper in the other to truly understand God's Word in our day. Many people today don't get their information about current events from the daily paper, but the basic idea still holds. We need to consider how the words of the prophets inform our social, political, and economic realities today. We need to hold up the prophets' mirror and see what it reflects to us, even if we don't like what we see.

I will briefly enumerate several key affirmations from the five prophetic writings we have studied. Take time to meditate on their meaning, even when they are challenging, for you, your congregation's life, and your responsibilities as a citizen.

God Communicates With Us, and We Can Experience God's Guidance for Our Lives and Our Communities

This is the basis for the prophetic word: God reveals God's vision to us in ways we can understand and connect with our political and personal lives.

God spoke to the prophets, working through them to guide a wayward people. Prophets condemned Israel and Judah for unfaithfulness and injustice, with the intent to inspire repentance and personal and national healing.

While God speaks through prophets, prophets don't have a monopoly on divine guidance. God says through the prophet Joel, "I will pour out my spirit upon everyone" (2:28). We can affirm that God continues speaking to God's people, giving us the wisdom we need to be God's healing companions.

God Is Concerned About the Details of Our Lives and Communities

Who we are and what we do really matters. Our lives matter to our loved ones and colleagues, but they also matter to God. We can affirm with the author of Psalm 139 that nothing is hidden from God: God has searched us and knows us completely. Our actions make a difference to God and bring beauty or ugliness to God's experience of the world. This is the message of the cross: Although God is victorious over death, God also experiences the suffering of Christ and all who cry out in pain and despair.

God Is Concerned About Justice in Our Personal and Corporate Lives

Amos, the earliest of the prophets, proclaims, "Let justice roll down like waters, and righteousness like an ever-flowing stream" (Amos 5:24). Micah 6:8 adds the following challenge: "What the LORD requires from you: to do justice, embrace faithful love, and walk humbly with your God." Justice and injustice matter to God.

I believe that Jesus saw himself as embracing and fulfilling the wisdom of prophetic tradition. The Gospels are the progression of prophetic insight and challenge in their affirmation of God's intimate love, "when you have done it for the least of these brothers and sisters of mine, you have done unto me" (Matthew 25:29). God's concern for justice embraces everything we do and inspires us to be God's companions as justice seekers.

God's knowledge of our lives is personal and intimate in such a way that God's joy and sorrow is related to our own and to the pain of the least of these. Will we do something beautiful for God or leave pain and ugliness in the wake of our lifestyle and corporate decisions?

Our Actions Have Consequences and Can Lead to Pain and Joy for Ourselves, Others, and the Institutions of Which We Are a Part

Some prophetic writings, following in the tradition of the Books of Deuteronomy and Leviticus, see both prosperity and adversity coming from the hand of God's response to our personal and institutional behavior. While God's direct role in causing natural and military devastation remains mysterious, we can affirm with the prophets that our acts shape the future of our communities and world for good or ill. Just and righteous actions promote life, while injustice and infidelity destroy relationships, lead to poverty and powerlessness, ravage nature, and produce crises between nations. Amos describes the dire consequences of unjust political and economic actions: "Doom to you who turn justice into a poison, and throw righteousness to the ground!" (Amos 5:7). But the prophet knows that all isn't lost and tells the people to "Seek the LORD and live" (Amos 5:6). What consequences will come from unrestrained materialism or neglect of the natural world or callousness toward the hungry and homeless? And how are we reaping what we've already sown?

We Have the Freedom to Repent, Change Course, and Follow God's Vision for Our Lives

Here the prophets provide the promise of hope in times of trial. Although our past behaviors and unjust social structures condition our lives and can limit our freedom and the freedom of others, the prophets are clear that we are not passive victims but creative actors in shaping our lives and history. Jonah highlights our freedom to change. Despite their evil actions, the people of Nineveh hear Jonah's message, repent, and call a fast. The city becomes a new creation, and God changes God's plan to destroy it. We can, as Hosea asserts, "Return to ... God with faithful love and justice, and wait continually with your God" (Hosea 12:6). We have the freedom to change our lives and to work to change the institutions of which we are a part. The prophetic promise is that when we repent of our sin, we see new possibilities for reconciliation and redemption. God hears our confessions and responds with grace, inspiration, and healing.

A God Who Feels the World

God's most radical expression of love for us was the incarnation. By becoming human in the person of Jesus, God showed us first hand the creative love that forgives sins, heals the sick, and challenges us to seek justice. In Jesus, God experienced human pain in real time; God wept over Jerusalem and at Lazarus's graveside; God showed compassion for the lost and entered into dialogue in the Temple, willing to be a student as well as a teacher. God knows us better than we know ourselves, and this intimate knowledge truly changes God's experience. God's constant love can heal and transform our lives.[1]

Even in Difficult Times, God's Involvement in History Gives Us Hope for the Future

God is involved in our lives now and in the future. God wants nations to flourish and live according to principles of justice. God is not finished with any one of us, and God is not finished with the world. We see in the writings of the prophets a lively dialogue between humanity and God in which human actions lead to new ways for God to transform the world. We see God have mercy on the people of Nineveh after they repent of their sins. And Joel tells us that "everyone who calls on the LORD's name will be saved" (Joel 2:32). Our hope is in a living, active God whose mercies are new every morning—a God who never gives up but constantly works for the redemption of humankind, individuals and nations alike.

God's Ultimate Goal Is Healing the Earth and Humanity

This is the heart of Jewish and Christian hope. The prophets' words seem harsh, but their intent is to bring the nation and its people back to God. An authentic relationship with God leads to justice and well-being for humans and animals alike. God's final words to Jonah, later embodied in the life and teachings of Jesus, give us hope still today: "Yet for my part, can't I pity [deeply love] Nineveh, that great city, in which there are more than one hundred twenty thousand people, who can't tell their right hand from their left, and also many animals?" (Jonah 4:11). God imagines a new world and will bring it about in God's good time.

Live the Story

The words of the prophets still ring true in our time. As followers of the prophetic Jesus, our faith calls us to shine like stars in the world by following a different set of values and priorities (Philippians 2:14). The prophets call us to a holistic faith and spirituality in which prayer is completed by acts of justice. There are plenty of threats to our well-being, many of which are consequences of our own decisions.

The prophetic message is concrete in its plea and challenge for us to repent and to transform our lives. We should act in ways that lead to life instead of devastation. To borrow an image from Martin Luther King, Jr., we can become a headlight, instead of a taillight, when it comes to responding to critical issues of our time.

After having lived with these five prophetic texts, how do you find their message of challenge and hope relevant to people in the twenty-first century? How will the prophets' words inspire you to change your way of life, priorities, and consumption patterns? How does your church need to change to be faithful to the prophets' message? What words of challenge do the prophets have for twenty-first century citizens and political institutions?

The prophetic word is ultimately about hope—hope in our ability to change, hope in the possibility of justice for the vulnerable, and hope in God's vision for history and humankind. This is an active hope that inspires us to commit ourselves to new behaviors and practices. In light of the prophetic word, what one hopeful first step can you make to change your life and your impact on the world?

---

1. For more on the vision of God as creative-responsive love, influenced by the world, see John B. Cobb and David Ray Griffin, *Process Theology: An Introductory Exposition* (Louisville: Westminster/John Knox, 1996) and Bruce Epperly, *Process Theology: A Guide for the Perplexed* (London: Continuum, 2011).

Leader Guide

People often view the Bible as a maze of obscure people, places, and events from centuries ago and struggle to relate it to their daily lives. IMMERSION invites us to experience the Bible as a record of God's loving revelation to humankind. These studies recognize our emotional, spiritual, and intellectual needs and welcome us into the Bible story and into deeper faith.

As leader of an IMMERSION group, you will help participants to encounter the Word of God and the God of the Word that will lead to new creation in Christ. You do not have to be an expert to lead; in fact, you will participate with your group in listening to and applying God's life-transforming Word to your lives. You and your group will explore the building blocks of the Christian faith through key stories, people, ideas, and teachings in every book of the Bible. You will also explore the bridges and points of connection between the Old and New Testaments.

Choosing and Using the Bible

The central goal of IMMERSION is engaging the members of your group with the Bible in a way that informs their minds, forms their hearts, and transforms the way they live out their Christian faith. Participants will need this study book and a Bible. IMMERSION is an excellent accompaniment to the Common English Bible (CEB). It shares with the CEB four common aims: clarity of language, faith in the Bible's power to transform lives, the emotional expectation that people will find the love of God, and the rational expectation that people will find the knowledge of God.

Other recommended study Bibles include *The New Interpreter's Study Bible* (NRSV), *The New Oxford Annotated Study Bible* (NRSV), *The HarperCollins Study Bible* (NRSV), the *NIV and TNIV Study Bibles*, and the *Archaeological Study Bible* (NIV). Encourage participants to use more than one translation. *The Message: The Bible in Contemporary Language* is a modern paraphrase of the Bible, based on the original languages. Eugene H. Peterson has created a masterful presentation of the Scripture text, which is best used alongside rather than in place of the CEB or another primary English translation.

One of the most reliable interpreters of the Bible's meaning is the Bible itself. Invite participants first of all to allow Scripture to have its say. Pay attention to context. Ask questions of the text. Read every passage with curiosity, always seeking to answer the basic Who? What? Where? When? and Why? questions.

Bible study groups should also have handy essential reference resources in case someone wants more information or needs clarification on specific words, terms, concepts, places, or people mentioned in the Bible. A Bible dictionary, Bible atlas, concordance, and one-volume Bible commentary together make for a good, basic reference library.

The Leader's Role

An effective leader prepares ahead. This leader guide provides easy to follow, step-by-step suggestions for leading a group. The key task of the leader is to guide discussion and activities that will engage heart and head and will invite faith development. Discussion questions are included, and you may want to add questions posed by you or your group. Here are suggestions for helping your group engage Scripture:

State questions clearly and simply.

Ask questions that move Bible truths from "outside" (dealing with concepts, ideas, or information about a passage) to "inside" (relating to the experiences, hopes, and dreams of the participants).

Work for variety in your questions, including compare and contrast, information recall, motivation, connections, speculation, and evaluation.

Avoid questions that call for yes-or-no responses or answers that are obvious.

Don't be afraid of silence during a discussion. It often yields especially thoughtful comments.

Test questions before using them by attempting to answer them yourself.

When leading a discussion, pay attention to the mood of your group by "listening" with your eyes as well as your ears.

Guidelines for the Group

IMMERSION is designed to promote full engagement with the Bible for the purpose of growing faith and building up Christian community. While much can be gained from individual reading, a group Bible study offers an ideal setting in which to achieve these aims. Encourage participants to bring their Bibles and read from Scripture during the session. Invite participants to consider the following guidelines as they participate in the group:

Respect differences of interpretation and understanding.

Support one another with Christian kindness, compassion, and courtesy.

Listen to others with the goal of understanding rather than agreeing or disagreeing.

Celebrate the opportunity to grow in faith through Bible study.

Approach the Bible as a dialogue partner, open to the possibility of being challenged or changed by God's Word.

Recognize that each person brings unique and valuable life experiences to the group and is an important part of the community.

Reflect theologically—that is, be attentive to three basic questions: What does this say about God? What does this say about me/us? What does this say about the relationship between God and me/us?

Commit to a lived faith response in light of insights you gain from the Bible. In other words, what changes in attitudes (how you believe) or actions (how you behave) are called for by God's Word?

Group Sessions

The group sessions, like the chapters themselves, are built around three sections: "Claim Your Story," "Enter the Bible Story," and "Live the Story." Sessions are designed to move participants from an awareness of their own life story, issues, needs, and experiences into an encounter and dialogue with the story of Scripture and to make decisions integrating their personal stories and the Bible's story.

The session plans in the following pages will provide questions and activities to help your group focus on the particular content of each chapter. In addition to questions and activities, the plans will include chapter title, Scripture, and faith focus.

Here are things to keep in mind for all the sessions:

Prepare Ahead

Study the Scripture, comparing different translations and perhaps a paraphrase.

Read the chapter, and consider what it says about your life and the Scripture.

Gather materials such as large sheets of paper or a markerboard with markers.

Prepare the learning area. Write the faith focus for all to see.

Welcome Participants

Invite participants to greet one another.

Tell them to find one or two people and talk about the faith focus.

Ask: What words stand out for you? Why?

Guide the Session

Look together at "Claim Your Story." Ask participants to give their reactions to the stories and examples given in each chapter. Use questions from the session plan to elicit comments based on personal experiences and insights.

Ask participants to open their Bibles and "Enter the Bible Story." For each portion of Scripture, use questions from the session plan to help participants gain insight into the text and relate it to issues in their own lives.

Step through the activity or questions posed in "Live the Story." Encourage participants to embrace what they have learned and to apply it in their daily lives.

Invite participants to offer their responses or insights about the boxed material in "Across the Testaments," "About the Scripture," and "About the Christian Faith."

Close the Session
Encourage participants to read the following week's Scripture and chapter before the next session.
Offer a closing prayer.

1. The Prophet as Mystic and Voice for God
Hosea—Jonah

Faith Focus

God takes the initiative to reach out to humanity.

Before the Session

Write the following words on a markerboard or on a large sheet of paper attached to the wall: *prophet* and *mystic*.

Claim Your Story

Refer everyone to the words written on the board or paper. Hand two slips of paper to each person, and ask everyone to write a definition of *prophet* on one slip and a definition of *mystic* on the other. Collect the slips and read aloud the definitions of each word. Compare these definitions to dictionary definitions of the two words: *prophet:* one who speaks for God or a deity; *mystic:* one who strives to transcend ordinary human knowledge and experience through spiritual practices. How do these definitions add to your understanding of what a prophet or a mystic is?

Then talk about whom in the world today we might describe as a prophet or a mystic. Who has a message that God wants or needs us to hear? Who sets an example for how to grow spiritually? What can we learn from the words and example of these people?

Enter the Bible Story

The prophets in this study—Hosea, Joel, Amos, Obadiah, and Jonah—are confident that God speaks to them and uses them to reach out to humanity. We see this in the verses listed on page 15, in which "The LORD's word" comes to these prophets. While the prophets themselves are certain that God has given them instructions and a message, the prophet has the challenge of convincing his or her audience that a message carries God's authority. For that matter, those receiving the message have to decide whether the prophet truly represents God.

Discuss with the group how we would know whether an idea or instruction comes from God or was invented by the messenger. The author confesses that he gets nervous whenever he hears someone say, "God told me" or "I heard God saying to me." Do members of your group also get nervous? How do we know when we can trust someone who claims to speak for God? If you were in Hosea or Joel's original audience, would you take his message at face value or would you be skeptical? Would you demand some sort of evidence or ask for credentials?

Ask the group whether they understood the author's discussion of the two extremes that prophetic spirituality avoids: pantheism and deism. Talk about where you have seen examples of pantheism (the idea that God and the universe are one and that God is the totality of all things) and deism (the idea that God is distant, a creator who gets things started but does not interact with the creation). What are the problems with each of these approaches to God? How does our understanding of God affect our understanding of prophecy and how God communicates through people?

Invite the group to read Hosea 11:1-12. What does this chapter say about God, God's relationship with God's people, and how God intervenes in the world? How do these verses show a God who is neither a god of pantheism nor a god of deism?

The God of the prophets is one who works through humans to intervene in human affairs. Based on what we know about the prophets and their message, how does God intervene and what are God's priorities?

Live the Story

If everyone were to claim to speak on God's behalf, there would be chaos. But even though God doesn't communicate to and through everyone the way God spoke through prophets such as Hosea and Joel, all of God's children can speak with a prophetic voice.

Talk about how God may be calling members of your group to speak with a prophetic voice about matters in your community or in the world. Are there matters that you or other members of your congregation are in a unique position to address? Are there needs in your community that are being overlooked?

Commit to spending time in prayer over the next week, asking God where your prophetic voice may be needed.

2. Theology, Ethics, and Politics in the Prophetic Writings

Hosea—Jonah

Faith Focus

God calls us to be agents of justice and righteousness.

Before the Session

You'll need a markerboard and markers. Look up some dictionary definitions of the word *covenant*.

Claim Your Story

Watch a video of Martin Luther King, Jr.'s "I Have a Dream Speech." (Make sure that the video is authorized and free to use in educational settings.) Pay attention to any biblical references or allusions that King makes.

In particular, look up Amos 5:24, which King was referencing when he said, "We will not be satisfied until 'justice rolls down like waters, and righteousness like a mighty stream.'" Read all of Amos 5 to put this verse into context. Why is God calling for justice and righteousness? With what practices and behaviors is God upset or unsatisfied?

Enter the Bible Story

The writer looks at five themes when discussing justice and righteousness in the books of the prophets: 1) creation and ethics, 2) covenant and ethics, 3) the ethics of blessing, 4) the prophetic challenge to the rich and powerful, and 5) the call to turn to God.

1) Ask the group to read Genesis 1:1–2:4. What does this account of Creation have to say about ethics? What does it say about how we treat one another? How does the idea that humans are created in God's image affect the work that we do as the church and as God's representatives in the world?

2) Talk about the word *covenant*. How do we use that word in our culture? What do we use it to describe?

God had a covenant relationship with the people of Israel, a relationship in which both parties had a responsibility to uphold the covenant. List on one side of a markerboard some of the Israelites' obligations to God as part of this covenant. On the other side, list God's obligations to the Israelites.

Then talk about how we, as Christians, are in a covenant relationship with God. What is our covenant like? What are the terms, and what are our obligations? How is it an "invitation to a new way of life, characterized by justice, equality, and care for the least of these," to quote page 28?

3) "Count your blessings" is a cliché that we often appeal to in our culture, especially when someone is feeling sorry for himself or herself. (As time permits, discuss whether members of the group abhor or appreciate the sentiment behind the phrase "count your blessings.") Look over the Scriptures related to blessing that the writer mentions: Genesis 12:1-3 (Abram); Genesis 28:13-15 (Jacob); and Numbers 6:23-27. What do these Scriptures say about blessing? What does it mean that we, as God's people, are "blessed to be a blessing"? How does that idea inform our behavior and policy?

4) The writer says, "The prophets recognized that the wealthy and powerful have primary responsibility for ensuring the well-being of the nation." We see this theme over and again in the books of the prophets, but it raises two questions. First, who are the wealthy and powerful? Second, what responsibility do the wealthy and powerful have to the rest of their nation? Discuss these two questions as they apply to the culture that the prophets were addressing, as they apply to the culture that the Social Gospel Movement was addressing, and as they apply to current-day American culture.

5) Turning toward God means turning away from those things that compete with God for our attention. List on a markerboard things that people tend to put before God. These may be items named by the prophets (such as *idols* or *success and leisure at the expense of others*) or anything that draws people today away from God. Go through the list and discuss what makes each item alluring. Why are these things so hard to turn away from? What does it take to turn away from these false gods and toward the true God?

Live the Story

Reflect on the writer's two closing questions: "How can you and your congregation avoid complacency and become prophetic agents of justice and righteousness in your community and around the world?" and "What injustices might you address so that justice will 'roll down like waters and righteousness like an ever-flowing stream' (Amos 5:24)?"

Talk about what your congregation is doing and could do to address injustice and to be a voice of righteousness in your community and in the world.

Close in prayer, asking God to open your eyes to ways that you and your congregation can be "prophetic agents of justice and righteousness."

3. Hosea: Divine Passion and Human Infidelity
Hosea

Faith Focus
As God's people, we must turn away from false gods and toward the God who created us, loves us, and desires a covenant relationship with us.

Before the Session
Find a copy of your denomination or congregation's marriage service. If possible have copies available for everyone in the group. (Do not make photocopies of materials unless these materials specifically legally allow you to do so.)

Claim Your Story
Search on a computer, phone, or tablet for the nearest Jewish temple or synagogue, mosque or Islamic center, Church of Jesus Christ of Latter-Day Saints congregation, Hindu temple, Buddhist temple, or Bahá'í center. If you live in an area with a large, religiously diverse population, you might look at how many of each house of worship are in your area, making note of the different varieties and sects that represent each faith. (You could also have one person find this information beforehand.)

Think about the people you know and often interact with who practice another faith, or no faith. What have you learned from these people about their religious beliefs and practices and about yours? How have your relationships with these people —or your lack of relationships with these people—shaped your understanding of the relationship between Christianity and other faiths?

Enter the Bible Story
This chapter looks at Hosea's marriage to the prostitute Gomer, which serves as a metaphor for God's relationship with Israel. Both a marriage and a relationship between God and God's people are covenants based on fidelity.

Invite married members of your group to tell stories of how they and their spouse came together. What sort of commitment did they make to each other and how did they make that covenant formal or official? If no one in your group is married, talk about couples in your congregation or families that exemplify what it means to be in a lifelong covenant relationship.

Then take a look at your denomination or congregation's official or preferred marriage service. (For example, if you are United Methodist, you would look at the "Services of Christian Marriage" in *The United Methodist Book of Worship*.) What vows do those getting married make to each other? What vows do they make to God? What does it look like for married persons to be faithful to each other and to their vows? What happens if someone in the relationship is not faithful?

When we look at God's relationship with Israel as a marriage, what vows has each party made? What responsibilities does each party have to this covenant relationship? Discuss how Israel failed to remain faithful to its vows and how God's responded to this infidelity.

Then talk about our relationship with God. What vows have we made to God? (You may choose to take a look at your denomination or congregation's services of baptism and membership.) What promises does God make to us?

The Kingdom of Judah's greatest crime was turning to foreign gods. In doing so, they violated their covenant with God. How does Judah's infidelity in Hosea inform our involvement with people and traditions of other faiths? The writer mentions on page 38 that Christians today "practice yoga and Tai Chi, and go to acupuncturists and Buddhist retreat centers." All of these practices have their origins in non-Christian faiths and spiritualities, although many have been detached from their origins and repackaged. Discuss whether these practices violate our covenant with God. If not, what are some other false gods (such as money or recognition) that you worship that cause you to be unfaithful to God.

As time and comfort level permit, go around the room or table and have each person name one god, other than God, that he or she is devoted to. You may choose to go around the table multiple times.

Live the Story

If we're honest with ourselves, we all, like the people of Judah, have been unfaithful to God. Hosea gives us hope. The Book of Hosea does not end with God's disappointment but with a plea for the people to return and a promise of God's love and healing.

Close by allowing everyone time to, silently or aloud, name one way he or she will turn toward God and away from whatever false gods he or she has been serving. Your group might come up with a plan for its members to hold one another accountable to these commitments, keeping tabs on one another during the week through e-mail or text messaging.

4. Joel: Repentance and Restoration

Joel

Faith Focus

God answers our prayers and responds to our actions.

Before the Session

Have on hand a markerboard and markers. Do some research on natural disasters that have struck during the past decade. Also find out which places in the world are facing hardship right now. Do your best to find examples that many people are not aware of.

Claim Your Story

Begin by making a list on a markerboard of major natural disasters that have happened in the last decade. This might include the 2010 earthquakes in Haiti and Chile, Hurricane Sandy in 2012, or the East African drought of 2011.

Then discuss each example and talk about God's role, and God's supposed role, in each of these disasters. The author gives an example in this chapter of a Christian pastor (namely John Piper) who suggested that God was using a particular disaster to send a message. When have you heard other Christian leaders make a similar point about a one of the natural disasters on your list? If we reject the idea that God uses forces of nature, such as earthquakes and hurricanes, in what way is God present amid these tragedies?

Enter the Bible Story

The big, underlying question in this chapter is, "Does God change?" Has God planned every detail of this world and our lives in advance, or does God change in response to what we do? The author describes on page 46 Joel's view of history as "the result of an ongoing divine-human call and response" in which "God can change God's attitude toward us, depending on our responses to the events of our lives."

Ask the members of the group to read Joel 2:1-32. In these verses, the prophet tells the people of Judah, who are facing dark days on account of their misdeeds, to repent and return to God because God might have a "change of heart" (verse 14). Then God takes pity on Judah and promises to restore and protect them.

Invite participants to imagine that they are part of Joel's original audience. They are hearing this message calling them to repent so that God might show compassion on them. What questions might they have for the prophet about God, how God works, and what God expects from Joel? Talk about how Joel might answer these questions.

Live the Story

Invite participants to read James 5:13-16, in which James writes, "The prayer of the righteous person is powerful in what it can achieve" (5:16b). How do you take James's words seriously? How do you fail to do so?

Refer to the list of tragedies from the first activity. Ask the group whether they remember praying about these tragedies right after they occurred. If so, what did they pray for? Did they ask God to intervene in a particular way? If so, how? How did they expect or hope for God to respond?

Discuss the question, "Does God change?" as it relates to our prayers and our actions. Raise additional questions such as "If God has determined everything already, what is the purpose of prayers of petition?" and "If not, can our prayers convince God to change the course of human events?"

Invite each person in the group to talk about what he or she prays about during his or her prayer time and how he or she prays for these things. Does he or she simply lift up these requests to God or ask that God intervene in a specific way? Discuss how our understanding of God's will and God's role in human affairs affects what we pray for and how we pray for these things.

Close by taking prayer requests (if you haven't already). Include in these prayer requests places around the world suffering from disaster and other hardship. Ask that God make God's presence known among those who are suffering and recovering from disaster, illness, or other struggles.

5. Amos: Spirituality, Ethics, and Economics
Amos

Faith Focus
God holds us accountable for the well-being of the most vulnerable people in our society.

Before the Session
Do some research on the Social Gospel movement of the early twentieth century. Gather information on ways your congregation is serving as an advocate for poor and vulnerable persons in your community.

Claim Your Story
The writer opens this chapter with a discussion of the difference between religion that focuses on the individual and religion that seeks justice. He includes a quotation from Walter Rauschenbush, who is credited with founding the Social Gospel movement.

The Social Gospel put an emphasis on faith that is practical and makes an impact on people's lives. Those who embraced a social gospel were concerned with issues such as poverty, income inequality, racism, alcoholism, inner-city living conditions, and public health. Do some research on the Social Gospel movement, its impact and legacy, and its critics. (It doesn't need to be heavy research.)

Talk about how the Social Gospel movement has had an impact on what the church does today, where the movement may have fallen short, and why it's important that we have a practical faith.

Enter the Bible Story
Prophets have a way of running afoul of those in positions of authority, whether political or religious authorities. Amos, who was from the town of Tekoa in the Southern Kingdom of Judah, spent much of his career in the Northern Kingdom of Israel. So he already had the disadvantage of being an outsider. Then he had the audacity to challenge Israel's great wealth and prosperity.

Discuss the popular sentiment "God bless America." (You might even hum or sing a verse of the song of the same name.) Talk about what it means for God to bless a nation or people. What sorts of things might we confuse for God's blessings (such as wealth or military strength)? Relate this discussion to what Amos faced in ancient Israel. How did the people there confuse their security and material wealth as blessings from God?

Israel during Amos's time may have appeared, on the surface, to be a model nation. But as the writer points out on page 55, all was not well: "The gap between the rich and poor had widened; people of modest means had little access to the legal system; poverty led to heads of households selling themselves into virtual slavery to pay off debts; and farms were being foreclosed upon." Talk about what injustices might be lurking under the surface in otherwise prosperous first-world countries today. Are there ways in which prosperity for some depends on exploiting others (including people in less prosperous nations)? Consider the wages and working conditions of those responsible for picking the fruits and vegetables you eat or for making the clothes that you wear.

With these things in mind, talk about God's "preferential option for the poor" (page 61). Be sure that everyone understands that having a preferential option for the poor does not mean that God loves poor people more than those who are financially privileged but that God is an advocate for those on the margins of society. Talk about how you see God's preferential option for the poor at work in Amos's writings.

Live the Story

What does God's preferential option for the poor mean for you, your congregation, and its ministries? Identify ways that your congregation is already an advocate for the most vulnerable people in your community. How are you serving those who are poor, hungry, homeless, ill, or imprisoned not only by helping to meet their basic needs but also by working to ensure that these people are treated justly and have opportunities to improve their situation, that the wider community is aware of their needs, and that they are treated with dignity.

Discuss what else you could do, as a group or a congregation, to respond to injustice in your community. Before you commit to anything, do some research on these problems and their causes. Also find out which churches and groups are already working to address these issues, and look for ways you could partner with them.

6. Obadiah: Justice, Punishment, and Hope
Obadiah

Faith Focus

We serve a God of justice and judgment, but we are not a people of revenge.

Before the Session

Read the entire Book of Obadiah. (It isn't very long.) Also do some research on the 2006 Amish school shooting in Lancaster County, Pennsylvania, particularly the community's response to the shooting. You will need half- or quarter-sheets of paper and pens or pencils.

Claim Your Story

This chapter opens with the story of the 2006 shooting at an Amish schoolhouse outside of Lancaster, Pennsylvania, in which the shooter, Charles Roberts, killed five children and wounded five others before committing suicide. The Amish community that suffered this tragedy surprised many by responding with forgiveness, going as far as to reach out to and set up a fund to support Roberts's family.

This community demonstrated the sort of radical forgiveness that Jesus expects from all of us. Begin your time together by talking about persons and groups who have been responsible for horrible tragedies and/or injustices in your community or nation. Have group members discuss their feelings toward these people or groups? Have they forgiven them? If so, does forgiveness mean forgetting what happened, or letting it go? Did group members want revenge? Do they still?

Before moving on, say a prayer for your community and nation and for those who have done your community and/or nation harm, as well as for those who wish to do so. Ask God for the strength and courage to offer forgiveness but also the wisdom to know how to respond to enemies who pose danger.

Enter the Bible Story

The Book of Obadiah is the only book of the Old Testament that has only a single chapter. Allow everyone the time to read the entire book. For context, explain that the people of Edom were believed to have been the descendants of Jacob's twin brother, Esau. (Israel traced its lineage back to Jacob himself, whom God renamed Israel.)

In your study of Amos, you discussed justice in the context of making things right, especially for the poor and vulnerable. Obadiah deals with justice of another sort: Israel wants to bring its neighbor Edom, which is guilty of "slaughter and violence," to justice. This justice involves retribution, to the point that "The house of Jacob will be a fire ... and the house of Esau straw; they will burn them up completely" (Obadiah 18).

Talk about God's role in this type of justice. Does justice of this sort allow for God's grace and mercy? Then talk about Israel's role. How were they to participate in bringing justice to Edom?

Compare the content of the Book of Obadiah to the messages of retribution and vengeance that you hear following an event such as a shooting or terrorist attack. Then challenge each person in the group to imagine how he or she would have received Obadiah's message. Would he or she have been reluctant to answer violence with violence? Or would he or she have cheered on Edom's punishment?

Live the Story

Hand out half- or quarter-sheets of paper, and make sure that everyone has a pen or pencil. Invite everyone to list on the paper those people or groups whom he or she feels animosity toward or holds a grudge against. (Group members may, instead, list these on a phone or tablet, using a note-taking application.) Suggest that everyone keep his or her list in his or her wallet, purse, Bible, phone, or other place where he or she can access it easily and frequently and take time each day to pray for the people he or she listed.

Close your time together by taking a look at Jesus' teaching on enemies from his Sermon on the Mount, Matthew 5:38-42, then at his teaching on forgiveness, Matthew 6:14-15. How do these teachings affect how we as Christians read Obadiah?

7. Jonah: When Grace Goes Beyond Justice
Jonah

Faith Focus
God has a way of challenging us and forcing us out of our comfort zone.

Before the Session
If possible, talk to someone involved with children's ministries at your church about teaching the story of Jonah to children. Talk about why this story seems to resonate with children and what parts of the story Christian education tends to emphasize when teaching the story to children. You will need scrap paper and pens or pencils.

Claim Your Story
The writer opens this chapter by saying, "Theology matters!" Sometimes we hear the word *theology* and think of it as some sort of academic discipline that isn't for laypeople. But theology is simply what we think and believe about God. Every person of faith is a theologian, though not every believer has a mature theology.

Hand out scrap paper, and make sure that everyone has a pen or pencil. Invite the members of the group to think about their theology: What do they believe about God and God's relationship to humanity and all of creation? Ask each person to list five phrases or short sentences he or she would use to describe God. As Christians, when we talk about God, we are talking about all three persons of the Trinity. So their descriptions may refer to Jesus Christ or the Holy Spirit.

Have the participants divide into pairs or groups of three to discuss their descriptions of God. Tell the members of each group or pair to read aloud their lists then to discuss the three situations the writer mentions in the "Claim Your Story" portion of this chapter: the family member who was convinced that an aunt and uncle were damned because of unorthodox beliefs, the 2011 doomsday predictions of Harold Camping and the well-meaning people who took them seriously, and the 9/11 terrorist attacks. In pairs or groups, have participants talk about how they would have responded in these situations, based on their understanding of God. (What would they have said to the cousin or to a friend who was selling everything to prepare for the end of the world? How would they have responded to the idea of nuking the terrorists?)

Enter the Bible Story
The story of Jonah is one of the best known in all of Scripture. It's one of those stories that many people learn as children. Have the group think back to when they first heard the

story of Jonah and how it was taught to them. Was the focus on Jonah's attempt to flee from God's call, on Jonah's time inside the fish, or on the repentance of Nineveh?

Then talk about why Jonah's story is so popular, especially with children, and why it is a story we like to teach children. What lessons do we want children to learn from Jonah, from his relationship with God, from his response to God's call, and from God's relationship with Nineveh?

Have the participants divide into groups of three or four. The groups should come up with a plan for teaching the Book of Jonah to children, in light of what they've learned from this chapter. They don't need to come up with teaching-and-learning activities for this hypothetical lesson (unless they really want to). They should decide what children most need to know and understand about the Book of Jonah and what children can take away from this story and apply to their lives. And they should think about how they would communicate these lessons in a way that a child could understand.

Have each group present its plan. Discuss how their plans are similar to and different from ways the Book of Jonah is commonly taught to children.

Then talk about what lessons from the Book of Jonah aren't for children. What new insights do we gain from reading this text as adults? How does a story about a prophet running from God and spending time inside a fish become a "theological masterpiece" (as the writer describes it) that challenges our understandings of grace and judgment? What do we miss out on when we stick with the children's version of the story?

Live the Story

Jonah struggles with God's will. He is reluctant to go to Nineveh when God first calls him. Later he is upset that God has spared the Ninevites. Being faithful to God doesn't mean getting our way. God will challenge us and force us out of our comfort zone.

Ask everyone to think of one way he or she has changed thinking as a result of his or her relationship with God. Have participants divide into pair or groups of three to talk about how God has changed their views, values, or beliefs and how these changes have affected their behavior and relationships with other people.

8. The Prophetic Challenge Today

Hosea—Jonah

Faith Focus

The words and vision of the biblical prophets are still relevant for God's people in the twenty-first century.

Before the Session

Gather one small mirror (makeup mirrors are fine) for each participant. Have on hand a markerboard and markers.

Claim Your Story

Hand everyone a mirror. Each person should look at his or her reflection in the mirror for things about himself or herself that he or she has not noticed before. This might include the shape of an ear, a freckle, or the way his or her hair is laying that day.

Have everyone name something he or she hadn't noticed before. Then talk about the value and role of mirrors. What would life be like without mirrors? Would we be less concerned about how we look, or would we be more anxious about our appearance? Discuss situations when mirrors seem essential, and discuss the dangers of spending too much time looking in the mirror.

Then discuss the questions that the author lists on page 82, reflecting on what you've read and learned from the first seven chapters:

- Where have the prophetic writings challenged your priorities and lifestyle?
- In what ways have they challenged the values and practices of our congregation?
- What changes would we have to make to be faithful to the prophetic message for our time? What changes would our community and nation need to make?

Enter the Bible Story

Review what you've learned and discussed during the previous seven sessions, considering each of the key affirmations the writer raises:

1) God communicates with us, and we can experience God's guidance for our lives and our communities. Divide a markerboard in half. List on one side all of the ways in which humans communicate with one another. List on the other side ways in which God communicates with humans. Compare and contrast the two lists. Talk about which forms of communication are most likely to get across message clearly and which are less reliable. Also discuss whether how certain types of communication allow the recipient to ignore or shut out the messenger. How do we, as God's people, ignore or shut out God?

2) God is concerned about the details of our lives and communities. Invite everyone to read Psalm 139:7-12. What does this Scripture tell us about God's presence, and how does it relate to how God works through the prophets? How does it show God's concern for all aspects of our lives?

3) God is concerned about justice in our personal and corporate lives. During the previous seven sessions, you've talked a lot about justice: justice among individuals, justice between nations, and justice between a nation and its most vulnerable citizens. Based on what you've learned and discussed, how do you determine what is just, or right? How do you determine whether a person or group is treated fairly and with dignity? Read Matthew 25:31-46. How do Jesus' words in this Scripture inform your understanding of justice? Divide participants into pairs or groups of three and invite them to talk about ways in which they, as individuals, can work toward justice.

4) Our actions have consequences and can lead to pain and joy for ourselves, others, and the institutions of which we are a part. Brainstorm a list of behaviors and characteristics that promote injustice—behaviors and characteristics such as materialism, apathy, and selfishness. List these on a markerboard. Go through the list and talk about the consequences of each of these actions and attributes, both for the individual and for his or her community.

5) We have the freedom to repent, change course, and follow God's vision for our lives. As a group, take another look at Jonah 3:1-10. The people of Nineveh took hold of that freedom and changed course. Repentance begins with confession. Allow for time in silence for participants to confess their sins before God. If your congregation or denomination says a prayer of confession each week in worship, you might close this time by reciting that prayer aloud.

6) Even in difficult times, God's involvement in history gives us hope for the future. Even prophets such as Joel who prophesied during dark and difficult times presented hope to God's people. Discuss the hope that you have for your community and for the world. How can you communicate this hope?

7) God's ultimate goal is healing the earth and humanity. Discuss how this truth shapes everything we say and do as God's people.

Live the Story

The writer concludes by asking how the prophets' message of challenge and hope is relevant to us in the twenty-first century. Discuss, either as an entire group or a smaller groups of three or four, the following three questions:

- What twenty-first century injustices would the prophets identify and warn us against?
- What false gods in the twenty-first century might the prophets tell us to turn away from?

• How might the prophets instruct us to bring about justice and turn toward God?
• How will the words of the prophets inspire you to change your actions, way of life, and priorities?

Close your time together by inviting each person to commit to one change in his or her life on account of what he or she has discovered in these five books. Also commit to one change you can make as a group.

CPSIA information can be obtained
at www.ICGtesting.com
Printed in the USA
LVHW041802290822
727100LV00003B/413